THEOLOGY FOR BEGINNERS

F.J. SHEED

THEOLOGY FOR BEGINNERS

IGNATIUS PRESS   SAN FRANCISCO

Original edition: © 1957
Sheed & Ward, New York

Cover art: *The Last Supper*, 1897 (oil on canvas)
Gaston de La Touche (1854–1913)
State Heritage Museum, St. Petersburg, Russia
Bridgeman Images

Cover design by John Herreid

Reprinted in 2017 by Ignatius Press, San Francisco
ISBN 978-1-62164-119-3
Library of Congress Control Number 2017932959
Printed in the United States of America ∞

The greater part of this book has appeared in the columns of some twenty or more diocesan weeklies, under the headline "Theology for the Layman". I take this occasion to thank the Editors for the generous hospitality of their columns. I must most especially thank Mr. Joseph A. Breig of the Cleveland *Universe Bulletin* who first suggested the idea of the Series.

—F. J. Sheed [1956]

CONTENTS

I

WHY STUDY THEOLOGY?

A couple of years ago I visited a town where I was to lecture. A young woman told me she was coming to my lecture, and then asked what it was to be about. I said, "The Blessed Trinity". She said, "Oh", and then after a distinct pause, "Ah well." In other words, if her bishop wanted her to listen to a lecture on the Blessed Trinity, she would listen to it: she hoped, doubtless, that she would do even harder things if her bishop called for them. The one thing that emerged most definitely was that she expected no joy. And in that she represented any number of millions of her fellow Catholics. As a body, we hope to go to heaven, which means spending eternity with the Blessed Trinity, and we expect the experience to be wholly blissful; but in the prospect of spending an hour with the Blessed Trinity here below, there is no anticipation of bliss.

The incident took me back thirty years. I was a boy, and I had remarked to a theologian how sad it was that a layman could not get a course in theology. He said, "But why should you study theology? You are not obliged to." In my new excitement over dogma, I was quite incapable of giving any lucid answer to his question why. I mumbled something to the effect that the truth would make me free, and I wanted to be free. I shall try now to answer that question of thirty years back.

In a way I am still hampered now as I was then by a feeling of the strangeness of having to make a case for anything so exciting and so joy-giving. But the joy and excitement of theological knowledge is like the joy and excitement of any other love—it cannot be explained to one who has not experienced it; it need not be explained to one who has. I shall keep, therefore, to the plainest of reasons. Truth is food and truth is light.

"Not on bread alone doth man live", said Christ Our Lord, quoting Deuteronomy to the Devil. Everybody knows the phrase, and most people tend to complete it according to their own fancy of what is most important to the hungry soul of man. But it had its own completion in Deuteronomy and Our Lord reminded the Devil of that too—"but by every word that proceedeth from the mouth of God". Revealed truth, then, is food. Now it is a peculiarity of food that it nourishes only those who eat it. We are not nourished by the food that someone else has eaten. To be nourished by it, we must eat it ourselves.

Truth is light too. Not to see it is to be in darkness, to see it wrongly is to be in double darkness. The greater part of reality can be known only if God tells us: doctrine is what He tells: lacking it, we lack light. To be stumbling along in the dark, happy in the knowledge that our guides can see, is not at all the same thing as walking in the light. It is immeasurably better than stumbling through the dark with blind guides, but it is poverty all the same.

It will be said that no Catholic can go wholly unnourished, for there is the Eucharist, or wholly in the dark, because of the truths that the Church does manage to get through to the least interested of her children. As to the Eucharist, this is most gloriously true, though even there a man will be helped by going as far into the doctrine as the Church can take him, that he may know better by what food his soul lives. But as to the truths, I am not at all so sure. Some monstrous shapes flit about the Catholic mind: I remember an educated Catholic who was asked how God could be in three Persons and answered, "God is omnipotent, and can be in as many persons as He likes"; and another who, having broken his fast and wishing to go to Communion, thought it would be all right provided he went to confession first; and having kept no record, I cannot tell the number of times I have heard the phrase, "The poor Holy Spirit, He is so neglected"—that is, He does not get much of our attention and must make out as best He can with the company of the Father and the Son!

Let us not labor this. A Catholic, thank God, never can be wholly unnourished or wholly in the dark. But he may be living an undernourished life in the half-dark, and that is a pity.

I cannot say how often I have been told that some old Irishman saying his Rosary is holier than I am, with all my study. I daresay he is. For his own sake, I hope he is. But if the only evidence is that he knows less theology than I, then it is evidence that would convince neither him nor me. It would not convince him, because all those rosary-loving, tabernacle-loving old Irishmen I have ever known (and my own ancestry is rich with them) were avid for more knowledge of the Faith. It does not convince me because while it is obvious that an ignorant man can be virtuous, it is equally obvious that ignorance is not a virtue; men have been martyred who could not have stated a doctrine of the Church correctly, and martydom is the supreme proof of love: yet with more knowledge of God they would have loved Him more still.

Knowledge serves love—it *can* turn sour of course and serve pride or conceit and not love, and against this we poor sons of Eve must be on our guard.

Knowledge does serve love. It serves love in one way by removing misunderstandings which are in the way of love, which at the best blunt love's edge a little—for example, the fact of hell can raise a doubt of God's love in a man who has not had his mind enriched with what the Church can teach him; so that he is driven piously to avert his gaze from some truth about God in order to keep his love undimmed. But knowledge serves love in a still better way—because each new thing learned and meditated about God is a new reason for loving Him.

Now a Catholic might still feel that all this is convincing enough, but that none of it is for him all the same: the Church does not command him to go deep into theology; if his soul is not getting all the food it might, it suffers no hunger pangs; the half-dark seems pretty light to him, he knows he loves God; and anyhow it is his own business.

Now insofar as a Catholic is satisfied with what he is getting, there is no more to be said. It *is* his business; at least it's not mine. But life is not only getting; it must be giving as well, and a Catholic can hardly be so easily satisfied, or satisfied at all, with what he is giving. The most obvious fact of our day is that we are surrounded by millions who are starved of food that Christ Our Lord wanted them to have—they are getting too small a ration of truth, and of the Eucharist no ration at all. We regret their starvation, of course, but we do not lose any sleep over it; which raises the question of whether we really appreciate the food we ourselves get from the Church. We should not take it so calmly if their starvation were bodily: for we do know the value of the bread that perishes.

If spiritual starvation is to be relieved, it must be largely the work of the laity, who are in daily contact with starvation's victims. We must come to an understanding of the great dogmas, so that we know them in themselves and in their power to nourish; we must bend every effort to mastering their utterance. Only thus can we relieve the starvation that now lies all about us. Once we see it, we see that we must set about it—primarily and overwhelmingly for the sake of these others, since it is intolerable that men should be perishing for want of truth that we could bring them. But not only for their sake. For our own sake too: for it is not good for us, or our children, to be the sane minority in a society that is losing contact with God.

This book will be concerned with theology as meeting the twofold need—the need of our own souls for the food and light and love of God that the great dogmas bring with them; and the need of men all about us, a need which can be met only if we meet it.

The reading of this, and indeed of all theological books, should be accompanied by the reading of Scripture. Without that, it is possible to obtain an accurate knowledge of the truths of revelation, but Scripture has a wonderful power of making the truths come alive in the soul: it is possible for a man to possess the truth, while yet the truth does not possess him! The Gospels must of course be read; after them, the Acts of the Apostles and some of Saint Paul's Epistles—especially I Corinthians, Galatians, Ephesians, Philippians and Colossians; not hastily, but sooner or later, the whole of Scripture must be read.

II

SPIRIT

Spirit Knows, Loves, Is Powerful

When I was very new as a street-corner speaker for the Catholic Evidence Guild, a questioner asked me what I meant by *spirit*. I answered, "A spirit has no shape, has no size, has no color, has no weight, does not occupy space." He said, "That's the best definition of nothing I ever heard." Which was very reasonable of him. I had given him a list of things spirit is not, without a hint as to what it is.

In theology, spirit is not only a keyword, it is *the* keyword. Our Lord said to the Samaritan woman, "God is a spirit." Unless we know the meaning of the word spirit, we do not know what He said. It is as though He had said "God is a—." Which tells us nothing at all. The same is true of every doctrine; they all include spirit. In theology we are studying spirit all the time. And the mind with which we are studying it is a spirit too.

We simply must know what it is. And I don't mean just a definition. We must master the idea, make it our own, learn to handle it comfortably and skillfully. That is why I shall dwell upon it rather lengthily here. Slow careful thinking here will pay dividends later. This book is not planned as a hand gallop over the field of revelation. It is an effort to teach the beginnings of theology.

We begin with our own spirit, the one we know best. Spirit is the element in us by which we know and love, by which therefore we decide. Our body *knows* nothing; it *loves* nothing (bodily pleasures are not enjoyed by the body; it reacts to them physically, with heightened pulse, for instance, or acid stomach; but it is the knowing mind that enjoys the reactions or dislikes them); the body *decides* nothing (though our will may decide in favor of things that give us bodily pleasure).

Spirit knows and loves. A slightly longer look at ourselves reveals that spirit has power, too. It is the mind of man that splits the atom: the atom cannot split the mind; it cannot even split itself; it does not know about its own electrons.

Spirit Produces What Matter Cannot

Mind, we say, splits the atom and calculates the light-years. It is true that for both these operations it uses the body. But observe that there is no question which is the user and which is the used. The mind uses the body, not asking the body's consent. The mind is the principal, the body the instrument. Is the instrument essential? *Must* the mind use it to cope with matter? We have evidence in our own experience of mind affecting matter directly. We will to raise our arm, for example, and we raise it. The raising of the arm is a very complicated anatomical activity; but it is set in motion by a decision of the will. And as we shall see, the direct power the human mind has over its own body, mightier spirits have over all matter.

This mingling of spirit and matter in human actions arises from a fact which distinguishes man's spirit from all others. Ours is the only spirit which is also a soul—that is to say the life principle in a body. God is a spirit, but has no body; the angels are spirits, but have no body. Only in man spirit is united with a body, animates the body, makes it to be a living body. Every living body—vegetable, lower animal, human—has a life principle, a soul. And just as ours is the only spirit which is a soul, so ours is the only soul which is a spirit. Later we shall be discussing the union of spirit and matter in man to see what light it sheds upon ourselves. But for the present our interest is in *spirit*.

We have seen that in us spirit does a number of things: it knows and loves, and it animates a body. But what, at the end of all this, *is* spirit?

We can get at it by looking into our own soul, examining in particular one of the things it does. It produces ideas. I remember a dialogue one of our Catholic Evidence Guild speakers had with a materialist, who asserted that his idea of justice was the result of a purely bodily activity, produced by man's material brain.

SPEAKER: How many inches long is it?
QUESTIONER: Don't be silly, ideas have no length.
SPEAKER: OK. How much does it weigh?
QUESTIONER: What are you doing? Trying to make a
             fool of me?
SPEAKER: No. I'm taking you at your word. What
             color is it? What shape?

The discussion at this point broke down, the materialist saying the Catholic was talking nonsense. It is nonsense, of course, to speak of a thought having length or weight or color or shape. But the materialist had said that thought is material, and the speaker was simply asking what material attributes it had. In fact, it has none; and the materialist knew this perfectly well. Only he had not drawn the obvious conclusion. If we are continuously producing things which have no attribute of matter, there must be in us some element which is not matter, to produce them. This element we call spirit.

Oddly enough, the materialist thinks of us as superstitious people who believe in a fantasy called spirit, of himself as the plain blunt man who asserts that ideas are produced by a bodily organ, the brain. What he is asserting is that matter produces offspring which have not one single attribute in common with it, and what could be more fantastic than that? We are the plain blunt men and we should insist on it.

Occasionally a materialist will argue that there are changes in the brain when we think, grooves or electrical discharges or what not. But these only accompany the thought, they are not the thought. When we think of justice, for instance, we are not thinking of grooves in the brain; most of us are not even aware of them. Justice has a meaning, and it does not mean grooves. When I say that mercy is kinder than justice, I am not comparing mercy's grooves with the stricter grooves of justice.

Our ideas are not material. They have no resemblance to our body. Their resemblance is to our spirit. They have no shape, no size, no color, no weight, no space. Neither has spirit whose offspring they are. But no one can call it nothing; for it produces thought, and thought is the most powerful thing in the world—unless love is, which spirit also produces.

Spirit Is Not in Space

We have now come to the hardest part of our examination of spirit. It will have much sweat and strain in it, for you, for me; but everything will be easier afterward.

We begin with a statement that sounds negative, but isn't. A spirit differs from a material thing by having no parts. Once we have mastered the meaning of this, we are close to our goal.

A part is any element in a being which is not the whole of it, as my chest is a part of my body, or an electron a part of an atom. A spirit has no parts. There is no element in it which is not the whole of it. There is no division of parts as there is in matter. Our body has parts, each with its own specialized function: it uses its lungs to breathe with, its eyes to see with, its legs to walk with. Our soul has no parts, for it is a spirit. There is no element in our soul which is not the whole soul. It does a remarkable variety of things—knowing, loving, animating a body—but each one of them is done by the whole soul; it has no parts among which to divide them up.

This partlessness of spirit is *the* difficulty for the beginner. Concentrate on what follows—a being which has no parts does not occupy space. There is hardly anything one can say to make this truth any clearer: you merely go on looking at it, until suddenly you find yourself seeing it. The most any teacher can do is to offer a few observations. Think of anything one pleases that occupies space, and one sees that it must have parts, there must be elements in it which are not the whole of it—this end is not that, the top is not the bottom, the inside is not the outside. If it occupies space at all, be it ever so microscopic, or so infinitesimally sub-microscopic, there must be *some* "spread". Space is simply what matter spreads its parts in. But a being with no parts at all has no spread; space and it have nothing whatever in common; it is spaceless; it is superior to the need for space.

The trouble is that we find it hard to think of a thing existing if it is not in space, and we find it very hard to think of a thing acting if it has no parts. As against the first difficulty we must remind ourselves that space is merely emptiness, and emptiness can hardly be essential to existence. As against the second we must remind ourselves that parts are only divisions, and dividedness can hardly be an indispensable aid to action.

As against both we may be helped a little by thinking of one of our own commonest operations, the judgments we are all the time making. When in our mind we judge that in a given case mercy is more useful than justice, we hardly realize what a surprising thing we have done. We have taken three ideas or concepts, mercy, justice and usefulness. We have found some kind of identity between mercy and usefulness: mercy is useful. This means that we must have got *mercy* and *usefulness* together in our mind. There can be no "distance" between the two concepts: if there were, they could not be got together for comparison and judgment. If the mind were spread out as the brain is, with the concept mercy in one part of the mind, and the concept usefulness in another, they would have to stay uncompared. The concepts *justice* and *usefulness* must similarly be together and some identity affirmed between them, the judgment made that justice is useful. That is not all. All three concepts must be together, so that the superior usefulness of mercy can be affirmed. The power to make judgments is at the very root of man's power to live and to develop in the mastery of himself and his environment. And the power to make judgments is dependent upon the partlessness of the soul: one single, undivided thinking principle to take hold of and hold in one all the concepts we wish to compare.

One further truth remains to be stated about spirit. It is the permanent thing, the abiding thing.

Spirit Is Always Itself

As we have seen, a steady gaze will show us that a being which has no parts, no element in it that is not the whole of it, cannot occupy space. Continue to gaze, and we see that it cannot be changed into anything else, it cannot by any natural process be destroyed. We have at last arrived at the deepest truth about spirit—spirit is the being which has a permanent hold upon what it is, so that it can never become anything else.

Material beings *can* be destroyed in the sense that they can be broken up into their constituent parts: what has parts can be taken apart. But a partless being lies beyond all this. Nothing can be taken from it, because there is nothing in it but its whole self. We can conceive, of course, of its whole self being taken out of existence. This would be annihilation. But just as only God can create from nothing by willing a being to exist, so only God can reduce a being to nothing by willing it no longer to exist: and for the human soul, God has told us that He will not thus will it out of existence.

A spiritual being, therefore, cannot lose its identity. It can experience changes in its relation to other beings—e.g., it can gain new knowledge or lose knowledge that it has; it can transfer its love from this object to that; it can develop its power over matter; its own body can cease to respond to its animating power and death follows for the body—but with all these changes it remains itself, conscious of itself, permanent.

The student to whom all this is new should keep on thinking over these truths, turning back to them at odd moments—on the way to work, in periods of insomnia. He should keep on looking at the relation between having parts and occupying space till he sees, really sees, that a partless being cannot be in space. He should keep on looking at the relation between having parts and ceasing to exist, till he sees as clearly that a partless being cannot ever be anything but itself.

We should try to bring together, to *see* together, all these separate truths about spirit. One way is to concentrate upon our own soul, the spirit we know best—wholly itself, forever itself, doing each thing that it does with its whole self. Yet the human soul is the lowest of spirits. The least of the angels is unimaginably superior in power (those baby angels, all cute and cuddly, which disfigure our children's books, have nothing to do with angels).

The philosophers tell us that angels could, so powerful are they, destroy our material universe if the mightier power of God did not prevent them—as that same power will prevent man from destroying it until God wills that it should end.

It is not enough to have learned what spirit is. We must build the knowledge into the very structure of our minds. Seeing spiritual reality must become one of the mind's habits. When it does, we have reached the first stage of maturity. Materialism, however persuasively argued, can no longer take hold on us. We may not always be able to answer the arguments, but it makes no difference. Materialism is repulsive; all our mental habits are set against it. It is as if a scientist were to produce arguments in favor of walking on all fours: we should find the idea repulsive; all our bodily habits would be set against us. That indeed is no bad comparison. The man who knows of the universe of spirit walks upright, the materialist hugs the earth.

III

THE INFINITE SPIRIT

God Is Infinite Spirit

We have known all our lives that God is not an old man with a beard (looking rather like Karl Marx, especially when the artist wanted to show God angry, as he often did). We have realized, too, that the more complex picture of an old man with a long beard, a young man with a short beard, and a dove, bears no resemblance to the Blessed Trinity: it is merely the artist doing his best. But getting rid of the pictures is of value only if, in their place, we develop a truer idea of God: otherwise we have merely a blank where the pictures used to hang.

God is a spirit. As a first step toward forming our idea of Him, we imagine our body away and see our soul existing and functioning bodiless: it is partless, spaceless, immortal; it knows, loves, decides, acts. And all these things are true of God. But our soul is not God's equal, it is only His image. For God is infinite: we are not.

We note the meaning of the word *infinite*. It is from the Latin *finis*, meaning an end or boundary or limit; the prefix *in* is negative; it means that there is no such thing in God as a *finis*. God is without limit or boundary or end. Whatever perfection there is, God has it totally. Apply this notion of limit to our own soul: it knows certain things but they are a mere drop in the ocean of things it doesn't know: its knowing is limited. So is its loving. So is its power. There are none of these limits in God—He is all-knowing, all-loving, all-powerful.

We shall return to these but only after looking again at the difference we mentioned first—namely, that the soul owes its existence to God. He brought it into existence, holds it in existence, could reduce it to nothing again (but He has told us He will not). To have no hold of one's own upon existence is the most limiting limitation of all, and marks the greatest difference between the finite spirit which is our soul and the infinite spirit which is God.

Bernard Shaw tells of asking a priest, "Who made God?" The priest, says Shaw, was thunderstruck, his faith shattered. Whether he committed suicide or merely left the Church Shaw does not tell. But the whole thing is ridiculous. Every student of philosophy has heard the question: and they all know that there *must* be a being which did not need to be made. If nothing existed except receivers of existence, where would the existence come from? In order that anything may exist, there must be a being which does not have to receive existence, a being which simply has it. God can confer existence upon all other beings, precisely because He has it in His own right. It is His nature to exist. God does not have to receive existence, because He *is* existence.

Now we understand the name God gave Himself. The story is in the third chapter of Exodus. God had appeared to Moses in the burning bush. When Moses asked Him His name, God said "I AM WHO AM. Thus shalt thou say to the children of Israel: He who is hath sent me to you." This is God's name for Himself, I AM. Our name for Him is HE IS. (The Hebrew word for this is Jahveh. The Jews, out of reverence, avoided writing God's name in full;

they wrote the consonants only, JHVH. Somebody in the thirteenth century made a bad guess at the missing vowels and produced the word Jehovah. Actually there is no such word.)

That is the primary truth about God. He is, He exists, with all that existence in its fullness can mean. We shall look deeper into that.

God Is Omnipresent and Eternal

"Where was God before the universe was created?"asks the street-corner heckler. His question breaks up nicely into two—Where was God when there wasn't any where? Where was God when there wasn't any when? Briefly, the answer is that the words *where* and *when* have no application to God at all. But if we are as brief as that, no one will see the answer.

"Where" means "in what place", which means "in what location in space". But God is a spirit, and a spirit does not occupy space; only bodies need space. Yet we do say that God is everywhere. How can He be everywhere if He is not in space at all?

Follow closely. Everywhere means where everything is. The phrase God is everywhere means that God is in everything. Clearly a spiritual being is not in a material being as water is in a cup. We must look for a different meaning for the word "in". A spiritual being is said to be where it operates, in the things that receive the effects of its power. My soul for instance is *in* every part of my body, not by being spread out so that every bodily part has a little bit of soul to itself, but because the soul's life-giving energies pour into every part of the body. Everything whatsoever receives the energy of God, bringing it into existence and keeping it there; that is the sense in which

God is omnipresent, is everywhere, in everything. It is no convenience for God of course. He does not need things. But they need Him, desperately.

We can now look at the second part of our heckler's question—"before the universe was created". Just as "where" is a word of space—and God is not in space—so "before" is a word of time—and God is not in time either.

What is time? Saint Augustine gave the superb answer, "I know what time is—provided you don't ask me." But he went on from there, and so must we. Time is the measurement of change. Things go on changing, and time measures the changes. A watch whose hands do not move will not tell the time—because time measures change! Where nothing changes, there is nothing for time to measure, so there is no time. Our material universe is continuously changing, and time belongs to it. God is changeless, so time has no meaning in relation to Him. We are in time, God is in eternity.

If this sort of thing is new to you, it may be difficult at first. Keep thinking it over. God is changeless because He is infinite. He has all perfections. He cannot lose any of them, so there is no past into which they can flow away. Nor is there any future from which new perfections can flow to Him. He has all perfections, in the present, *a present which does not change and does not cease*. That is eternity. The universe He created is not like that. Things come and go. Change is continuous. *Time and the universe started together.*

We must concentrate upon the concept of eternity; it brings us deep into the meaning of God. You and I and all men are in time: which means that we are never at any moment the whole of ourself. What we were last year, what we will be next year, all belongs to our total being; but last year has gone and next year has not arrived. There never is a moment when we are all there. We possess our being, the philosophers say, successively. Not so God. All that He is, He possesses in one single act of being. Eternity does not mean everlasting time, time open at both ends, so that however far you go back into the past there is no beginning, however far you go forward into the future, there is no end. Eternity is not time at all. It is God's total possession of Himself.

Infinity, omnipresence, eternity—these are rich and rewarding concepts, but we should not stay with them too long at a time without returning to the Gospels to meet the living God. Christ is there for us, "whom", as Saint John says at the opening of his first Epistle, "we have seen with our eyes, whom we have looked upon, whom our hands have handled." The Infinite we are studying is the same Infinite whom we meet in the Gospels, the same Infinite whom we receive in the Blessed Eucharist. It may be well to repeat here what I said earlier. Gospel reading should accompany the reading of this book: without it, the theology we learn may be accurate but will not come properly alive in us. The Acts of the Apostles and some, at least, of Saint Paul's Epistles—1 Corinthians, for instance, Galatians, Ephesians, Philippians, Colossians—should follow the Gospels immediately. Then the rest of the New Testament and the Old in due course.

God's Knowledge, Love, Power

God, we have seen, is utterly changeless. This might strike us as involving Him in infinite stagnation. For us, with our matter-bound habits, activity seems unthinkable without change; but this, as we see looking closer, is because we are finite.

The first great activity of the infinite Spirit is knowing; with us this activity involves an immensity of change, learning what we had not known, forgetting what we had; in both cases the change comes from our finiteness, in the one case from ignorance, in the other from a defect of memory; but God knows all things, merely by being God, and there is no forgetfulness for Him; so that His activity of knowing is at once limitless and changeless; He is omniscient.

His other great activity is loving; and that again for men involves change, waxing and waning, finding new objects, losing hold upon things already loved; here again the change comes from our limitations; God loves with infinite loving-power: no loss possible, no increase conceivable. He knows and loves with infinite intensity, and this is not stagnation but measureless vitality.

God is all-powerful, too. There are no limits to what He can do, no limits to what He can make. The most powerful man cannot make anything of nothing at all, he needs *some* material to work upon, and in the absence of material his power must lie all locked up within him and unusable. That is a solid limitation and God lacks it. He needs no material: He creates.

"Can God make a weight so heavy that He cannot lift it?" asks the unbeliever. He feels he has us cornered. If we say "yes", then God cannot lift it; if we say "no" then God cannot make it. (The reader might do well to pause here and think out how he would answer it.) Our reply is that God can indeed do all things, but a self-contradiction is not a thing. God cannot make a four-sided triangle, because the terms contradict each other and cancel out: a four-sided triangle is meaningless; it is not a thing at all, it is nothing. A weight that an almighty Being cannot lift is as much a contradiction in terms as a four-sided triangle. It too is nothing. And (to give an old text a new emphasis) nothing is impossible to God.

Because God is infinite, there is no distinction between His attributes and Himself. This is difficult to put briefly. We must try. Take knowledge, and begin with our own. My knowing is something that I do, but it is not myself. This may not strike us as a limitation but it is, and a considerable one. If only my knowledge were myself, I should be knowing all the time, simply by being; I should not have to make a distinct effort to know; I should never forget. But, as it is, my knowledge is less than myself; I am finite enough, heaven knows, but my knowledge is more finite still.

Now God's knowing is not subject to this limitation. It is not distinct from Himself. It is Himself. If it were not, if there were really a distinction between His knowledge and Himself, then He would have something that His knowledge lacked. In that event it would not be infinite, and we should have to face the monstrosity of an infinite God with limited knowledge.

This applies to all His attributes—just as God *is* knowledge, so He is love, He is justice, He is mercy. We have to think of them as distinct, in order to think of them at all; but in Him they are not distinct from His very self, and therefore not from one another. Whatever God has, He is. And these attributes are not less themselves for being infinite. God's love would not be greater by being distinct from His very self—as ours is!

It is a difficult idea for our minds. But then God *must* be mysterious to the beings He made of nothing. Live with it; keep it in the mind; and our feeling that the attributes must be distinct will grow less, we shall begin to "see" their oneness in God.

We are now clearer, I hope, as to what God is. We are ready for the question: what is God's *life*, what does He do with Himself? We are ready, in other words, for the great adventure of the Blessed Trinity.

IV

THE BLESSED TRINITY

Three Persons

God is a living God. But what does His *life* consist of? It is hard to phrase the question, so little accustomed are we to thinking about this particular matter. Just as we ask what a man does with his time, so we may ask: What does God do with His eternity? What does He do with Himself? He is not infinitely idle: What is His life-work?

We might be tempted to say that He runs our universe, and leave it at that. But, of course, we cannot leave it at that. Running a finite universe could never be the whole life-work of an infinite Being. The universe seems vast to us; it is not vast to Him. He made it of nothing; He need not have made it at all. We may think of it as a sideline for God, not the main thing. If one were to describe Shakespeare as an actor, it would be true but it would leave out his supreme work, which was the writing of plays. That God runs our universe is true; but that *could* not be His life-work. What is?

Let us concentrate on the two great operations of spirit. God knows infinitely and loves infinitely. What does He love with His infinite loving-power? Almost instinctively we answer "Man". And this, thank God, is true. But, for the reason we have already seen, it cannot be the main truth. Finite creatures are no adequate object for infinite love—we cannot comprehend it, we cannot return it: and, once again, we need not have existed. Is infinite love never to find an object worthy of it?

We might say that God loves Himself; but, whatever light this might bring to the great theologian, there would be something a little depressing in it for the average Christian: the notion of God, solitary in eternity, loving Himself with all His might would not stimulate our own spiritual lives much. And indeed mankind has almost invariably found something frightening in the solitary God; it was to escape from that fear that the pagans invented their many gods. A God with companions of his own sort was not so frightening.

Their desire to find companionship for God was a true insight; their solution was wrong. It was left to Christ Our Lord to reveal to us that there is companionship *within* the one divine Nature—not a number of gods, but three Persons within the one God. It is in the knowledge and love of the three Persons that the divine life is lived. And Christ Our Lord wants to admit us to the knowledge of it.

As we read the Gospels, we find Our Lord saying something new about God—there are hints and foreshadowings of it in the Old Testament, but certainly no statement. Alongside His insistence that God is one, there is a continual reference to some sort of plurality. There is no watering-down, of course, of the strictest monotheism— Our Lord quotes from the Old Testament: "Hear, O Israel, the Lord thy God is one God." But there is a new element of more-than-oneness, which still leaves the oneness utterly perfect.

Matthew (11:27) and Luke (10:22) give us one phrase: "No one knoweth the Son but the Father; and no one knoweth the Father but the Son . . .": here are two persons put on one same level. "I and the Father are one" (Jn 10:30): they are two persons, yet one.

At the very end of Saint Matthew's Gospel, a third is brought in, still within the oneness—"Baptizing them in the name of the Father, and of the Son, and of the Holy Spirit"—three persons, but with one name, and therefore one nature, since God names things for what they are.

This combination of one and more-than-one is most fully evident in the four chapters—fourteen to seventeen—in which Saint John tells of the Last Supper. (Everyone who is beginning to take theology seriously should read those chapters again and again; there is no exhausting their richness.) What is especially to be noticed is a kind of "interchangeableness".

Thus when Philip the Apostle says (Jn 14:8), "Let us see the Father", Our Lord answered: "Whoever has seen Me has seen the Father."

Similarly Our Lord says that He will answer our prayer (Jn 14:14) and that His Father will (Jn 16:23); that He will send the Holy Spirit (Jn 16:7) and that His Father will (Jn 14:16).

In the doctrine of the Blessed Trinity all these phrases fall miraculously into place.

The Doctrine Outlined

The notion of one God who is three Persons must be profoundly mysterious. We could not know it at all if God had not drawn aside the veil that we might see. Even when He has told us, we might be tempted to feel that it was altogether beyond us. But it cannot be wholly dark. God would not mock us by revealing something of which we could make nothing at all. Since He wants to be known by us, we must respond by making the effort to know Him.

In its barest outline, the doctrine contains four truths:

(1) In the one divine Nature, there are three Persons, the Father, the Son and the Holy Ghost.
(2) No one of the Persons is either of the others, each is wholly Himself.
(3) The Father is God, the Son is God, the Holy Spirit is God.
(4) They are not three Gods but one God.

I once heard a theologian (not of our Faith) say, when someone asked him about the Trinity: "I am not interested in the arithmetical aspect of the deity"; even Catholics sometimes appear to think that we have here a mathematical contradiction, as if we were saying "Three equals one." We are not, of course. We are saying Three *Persons* in one *Nature*. The trouble is that, if we attach no meaning to the words *person* and *nature*, they tend to drop out; so we are left with the two numbers, as though they represented the supreme truth about God. We must see what person means and what nature means; then see what we can make of the three and the one.

The first stages of our investigation into person and nature are simple enough. We use the phrase "my nature", which means that there is a person, "I", who possesses a nature. The person could not exist without the nature, but some distinction there seems to be—the person possesses the nature, not vice versa. We say "my nature", not "nature's me".

Further we see that person and nature answer two different questions. If we are aware (in a bad light, say) that there is something in the room, we ask, "What is it?" If we can see that it is a human being, but cannot distinguish the features, we ask, "Who is it?" "What" asks about the nature, "who" asks about the person.

There is another distinction which calls for no special philosophical training to see. My *nature* decides what I can do. I can raise my hand, for instance, because that action goes with human nature; I can eat, laugh, sleep, think, because each of these actions goes with human nature. I cannot lay an egg, because that goes with bird nature; if I bite a man, I do not poison him, because that goes with snake nature; I cannot live underwater, because that goes with fish nature. But though it is my nature which decides what actions are possible to me, *I* do them, I the person; nature is the source of our operations, person does them.

Applying this beginning of light to the being of God, we can say that there is but one divine Nature, one answer to the question "What is God?", one source of the divine operations. But there are three who totally possess that one nature. To the question "Who are you?" each of the three would give His own answer, Father or Son or Holy Spirit. But to the question "What are you?" each could but answer "God", because each totally possesses the one same divine nature, and nature decides *what* a being is.

Because each possesses the divine nature, each can do all that goes with being God. Because each is God, there is no inequality, either in being or operation. It is necessary here to be accurate, upon two points especially.

First, the three Persons do not *share* the divine Nature; it is utterly simple and cannot be divided up; it can be possessed only in its totality.

Second, the three Persons are distinct, but not separate. They are distinct, because each is Himself; but they cannot be separated, for each is what He is solely by possessing the one same nature; apart from that one nature, no one of the Persons could exist at all.

At first, all this may seem dry and unrewarding. But only at first. The rewards for persistence are immense.

Mystery, Not Contradiction

The one, infinite, indivisible Nature of God is wholly possessed by three Persons—each of them, therefore, God, each of them, therefore, able to do all that goes with being God. If we are seriously using our minds upon this supreme truth, two difficulties may strike us: (1) it may seem quite inconceivable, practically a contradiction in terms, that one nature should be possessed by three persons; (2) we may feel that if the Father is God, the Son is God, and the Holy Spirit is God, then there are three Gods, not one.

We must look closely at each of these.

Take first the apparent impossibility of three persons having one single nature.

As we think of person and nature in ourselves, it seems clear that one nature can be possessed and operated in by only one person. But this apparent clearness comes from not looking deep enough. It is true that we are conscious of a reality within us, nature, by which we are *what* we are, and a reality within us, person or self, by which we are *who* we are. But whether these are two realities, or two levels or aspects of one reality, we cannot see with any certainty.

When we try to look really closely at ourselves, it is not so easy. Of our nature we have a shadowy notion, of our self a notion more shadowy still. When someone says "Tell me about yourself", we talk of our qualities or the things we do, but not of the *self* that has the qualities and does the things. We know there is a self there, the thing that says I, but we cannot get it into focus. Both as to the nature I have and the person I am there is more darkness than light.

So that although all our experience is of one nature being possessed by one person, we cannot honestly say that we know enough even of person and nature in man to assert that one to one is the only possible relation. Of the infinite being we have no experience at all: if God tells us that in Him there are three Persons, we have no reason to question, we must simply try to understand.

Now for the objection—the commonest of all from the intelligent atheist—that if each of the three Persons is God, then there must be three Gods. Perhaps the quickest way to show the fallacy here is to take the phrase "three men". Brown and Jones and Robinson are three distinct persons each possessing human nature. So far, as you say, there is a complete parallel. Father, Son and Spirit are three distinct persons, each possessing divine nature.

But observe the difference. Brown and Jones and Robinson each has his own allotment of human nature: Brown does not understand with Jones' intellect; Jones does not love with Robinson's will: each has his own. The phrase "three men", then, means three distinct persons, each with his own separate human nature, his own separate equipment as man.

The phrase "three Gods" could only mean three distinct persons, each with His own separate divine nature, His own separate equipment as God. But this is not so. They possess one single nature; they do in fact what our three men could not do—they know with the same intellect, love with the same will. They are three Persons and each is God; but they are one God, not three.

If this were all, we could say that at least we saw no contradiction in the doctrine of the Blessed Trinity. But we should probably say that we saw nothing else either. To learn that the infinite divine nature, already mysterious enough to us, is possessed by three entities more mysterious still, merely triples the darkness. It is in learning about the personalities of the Persons that we begin to find ourselves growing in the light.

We must, God aiding, bring our minds to bear upon that infinite act of generation by which God the Father begets His Son; and upon that infinite union in love by which the Holy Spirit proceeds from Father and Son. With that we are coming nearer the answer to our question—in what does God's life consist?

V

THE THREE PERSONS

Father and Son

The heavenly Father has a Son; the Gospels are full of their relation. We must now look at it more closely.

A son is a distinct person from his father; there is no way in which a father can be his own son. But though they are distinct persons, they are like in nature—the son of a man is a man, of a lion a lion. In this solitary case, the Father's nature is infinite; so the Son too must have an infinite nature. But there cannot be two infinite natures—one would be limited by not being the other and by not having power over the other. Therefore, since the Son has infinite nature, it must be the same identical nature as the Father's.

This truth, that Father and Son possess the one same nature, might remain wholly dark to us if Saint John had not given us another term for their relation—the Second Person is the WORD of the First. In the first eighteen verses of his Gospel we learn that God has uttered a Word, a Word who *is* God, who is in the bosom of the Father, by whom all things are made, who became flesh and dwelt among us.

God then utters a Word—not framed by the mouth, of course, for God has no mouth, He is pure spirit. So it is a word in the mind of God, an Idea. It is the Idea He produces of Himself. The link between having a son and having an idea of oneself is that both are ways of producing likeness; your son is like in nature to yourself; your idea of yourself bears some resemblance to you too—though it may be imperfect, for we seldom see ourselves very clearly; too many elements are seen wrong, too many not seen at all.

But the Idea that God has of Himself cannot be imperfect. Whatever is in the Father must be in His Idea of Himself, and must be exactly the same as it is in Himself. Otherwise God would have an inadequate Idea of Himself, which would be nonsense. Thus, because God is infinite, eternal, all-powerful, His Idea of Himself is infinite, eternal, all-powerful. Because God is God, His Idea is God. "In the beginning was the Word, and the Word was with God. And the Word was God."

So far, the reader may feel that all this is still rather remote—full of significance, no doubt, to theologians, but not saying much to the rest of us. With the next step we take, that feeling must vanish. The Father knows and loves; so His Idea knows and loves. In other words the Idea is a person. Men have ideas, and any given idea is something: God's Idea of Himself is not something only, it is Someone: for it can know and love.

The Thinker and the Idea are distinct, the one is not the other, Father and Son are two Persons. But they are not separate. An idea can exist only in the mind of the thinker; it cannot, as it were, go off and set up in business on its own. The Idea is in the same identical nature; we could equally well say that the nature is in the Idea, for there is nothing that the Father has which His Word, His Son, has not. "Whatsoever the Father has, that the Son has in like manner" (Jn 16:15). Each possesses the divine nature, but each is wholly Himself, conscious of Himself as Himself, of the Other as Other.

One immediate difficulty presents itself. We can hardly help thinking of sons as younger than their fathers. Is the Second Person younger than the First? If not, how can He be His Son? But this is another of those points where we must not argue from the image to the original. Among men, fathers are always older than sons simply because a human being cannot start generating the moment he exists; he must wait till he develops to the point where he can generate. But God has not to wait for a certain amount of eternity to roll by before He is sufficiently developed! Eternity does not roll by; it is an abiding Now; and God is infinite in all perfections, not needing to develop. Merely by being God, He knows Himself with infinite knowing power, and utters His infinite self-knowledge in the totally adequate Idea of Himself which is His co-eternal Son.

Holy Spirit

The production of a Second Person does not exhaust the infinite richness of the divine nature. Our Lord tells us of a Third Person. There is a Spirit, to whom Our Lord will entrust His followers when He Himself shall have ascended to the Father. "I will ask the Father and He will give you another Paraclete, that He may abide with you" (Jn 14:16). The Spirit, like the Word, is a person, He, not It. "But the Paraclete, the Holy Spirit, whom the Father will send in my name, He will teach you all things" (Jn 14:26).

As we have already seen, there is one huge and instant difference between God's Idea and any idea we may form. His is Someone, ours is only something. With an idea which is only something, there can be no mutuality: the thinker can know it, it cannot know him; he can admire its beauty, it cannot admire his; he can love it, it cannot return his love. But God's Idea is Someone, and an infinite Someone; between Thinker and Idea there is an infinite dialogue, an infinite interflow. Father and Son love each other, with infinite intensity. What we could not know, if it were not revealed to us, is that they unite to express their love and that the expression is a third Divine Person. In the Son, the Father utters His self-knowledge; in the Holy Spirit, Father and Son utter their mutual love.

Their love is infinite; its expression cannot be less. Infinite love does not express its very self finitely; it can no more produce inadequate expression than infinite knowledge can produce an inadequate Idea. Each gives Himself wholly to the outpouring of His love for the Other, holding nothing back—indeed the very thought of holding back is ridiculous; if they give themselves at all, they can give themselves only totally—they possess nothing but their totality! The uttered love of Father and Son is infinite, lacks no perfection that they have, is God, a Person, Someone.

As the one great operation of spirit, knowing, produces the Second Person, so the other, loving, produces the Third. But be careful upon this—the Second proceeds from, is produced by, the First alone; but the Third, the Holy Spirit, proceeds from Father and Son, as they combine to express their love. Thus in the Nicene Creed we say of Him "*qui ex patre filioque procedit*"—who proceeds from the Father and the Son; and in the *Tantum Ergo* we sing to Him "*procedenti ab utroque*"—to Him who proceeds from both.

We have seen the fitness of the names Son and Word for the Second Person. Why is the Third called Spirit?

Here the word Spirit—like the old English Ghost—is best understood as "breath". This is the root meaning; our ordinary word spirit comes from it, because spirit is invisible, as air is. It is in its root meaning that Spirit is the name of the Third Person—He is the "breath" or "breathing" of Father and Son.

That is Our Lord's chosen name for Him: and it is more than a name used merely because He has to be called something! There is some deep meaning in it. For Christ breathes upon the apostles as He says, "Receive ye the Holy Spirit"; when the Holy Spirit descends upon them at Pentecost, there is at first the rushing of a mighty wind.

We may wonder why the Third Person who is the utterance of the love of Father and Son should be called their Breath.

Let us note two things. It is of universal experience that love has an effect upon the breathing, it is a simple fact that the lover's breath comes faster. And there is a close connection between breath and life—when we stop breathing, we stop living. In the Nicene Creed the Holy Spirit is called "the Lord and giver of life". The link between life and love is not hard to see, for love is a total self-giving, and so a giving of life.

One final reminder. We saw how the Second Person is within the same nature, as an idea is always within the thinker's mind. So with the Third Person; the utterance of love by Father and Son fills the whole of their nature, producing another Person, but still within the same identical divine nature. Try to see the nature of God wholly expressed as Thinker, wholly expressed as Idea, wholly expressed as Lovingness.

Equality in Majesty

The truths God has revealed to us of His innermost life are not easy for us to take hold of and make our own. They do not yield much of their meaning at a first glance. I can only urge readers to go back over the last sections many times. Remember that we are making this study not to discover whether there are three Persons in God (for He has revealed that there are); still less to verify it (for no effort of our mind could make it any surer than God's own word); but simply to get more light on it and from it.

It is hardly my place to urge readers to pray for understanding. I can only state the plain fact that without prayer there will be precious little understanding. Our minds cannot take God's inner life by storm; we shall see as much as He gives us light to see.

But while we are talking of prayer, it should be noted that there is special light to be got from the Church's prayers, if we try to bring our new knowledge of the doctrines into saying them. The Preface of the Blessed Trinity in the Mass, for instance, is a blaze of meaning; so are the Creeds and some of the great hymns, especially the *Veni Sancte Spiritus* and the *Veni Creator*. No book on doctrine will teach you as much as the Missal—provided you bring some knowledge with you. That is why this book exists.

With what has gone before reread and meditated, we can go on to the completion of a first rough sketch of the doctrine of the Blessed Trinity.

We have already glanced at the erroneous idea that if God has a Son, the Son must be younger; Father and Son are co-eternal. Father, Son and Holy Spirit likewise are co-eternal. We must be on guard against thinking that *first* the Father had a Son, *then* Father and Son united to produce the Holy Spirit—and who knows what person may next emerge within the infinite fecundity of God? There is no question of succession, for there is no succession in eternity. The Father did not have to wait until He was old enough or mature enough to beget a Son or lonely enough to want one. He eternally *is*, in the plenitude of life and power. Merely by being, He knows Himself with that infinite intensity of knowledge which necessarily produces the Idea, the Son.

Nor must Father and Son wait while their love grows to the point where it can utter itself in a Third Person. Merely by being, they love with the plenitude of loving-power, merely by loving thus intensely they utter their love: the Holy Spirit is as inevitable as Father and Son.

We have used the words "necessarily" and "inevitably". They are worth a closer look. It is possible that the Son may seem less real to us because He is an Idea in the mind of His Father. He is, we may feel, only a thought after all, whereas we ourselves are not simply thoughts in God's mind; we really exist. But we exist only because God wills us to exist; if He willed us not to exist, we should cease to be.

But He cannot will the Second Person out of existence, any more than He willed Him into existence. We must not imagine the Father feeling that it would be nice to have a son and thinking one into existence, and as liable to think Him out of existence again if the humor took Him. It is an exigency of the divine nature that the Father should thus know Himself; simply by being Himself the Father knows Himself, generates the Idea of Himself; there is no element whatever of contingency in the existence of the Second Person; there is origin but no dependence. God is as necessarily Son as He is Father.

The same line of thought shows us the Holy Spirit, too, as necessarily existing. There is no difference among the Three in eternity or necessity; and there is no inequality. The Father possesses the divine nature unreceived; Son and Holy Spirit possess it as received; but they possess it in its totality. They have received everything from the Father, *everything*. To quote from the Preface for the Trinity:

"Whatever we believe, on Thy revelation, of Thy glory, we hold the same of the Son, the same of the Holy Ghost, without any difference to separate them. So that in the affirmation of the true and eternal Godhead, we adore distinction in the Persons, oneness in the Essence, equality in majesty."

Appropriation

The distinction of action among the Persons of the Blessed Trinity is a fact of the *inner* life of God. It is within the divine nature that each lives, knows, loves, as Himself, distinct.

But the actions of the divine nature upon created beings—ourselves for example—are the actions of all three Persons, acting together as one principle of action. It is by Father, Son and Holy Spirit that, for example, the universe is created and sustained in being, that each individual soul is created and sanctified in grace. There is no external operation of the divine nature which is the work of one Person as distinct from the Others.

Yet Scripture and Liturgy are constantly attributing certain divine operations to Father *or* Son *or* Holy Spirit. In the Nicene Creed, for instance, the Father is Creator, the Son is Redeemer, the Holy Spirit is Sanctifier, giver of life. That the Son should be called Redeemer is obvious enough: He did in fact become man and die for our salvation.

But since all three Persons create, why is the Father called Creator? Since all three Persons sanctify, why is the Holy Spirit called Sanctifier? Why—to use a theological term—is creation *appropriated* to the one, sanctification to the other?

If there is to be appropriation, of course, we can see why it is done like this: we can see, in other words, how these particular appropriations are appropriate. Within the divine Nature, the Father is Origin; Son and Holy Spirit both proceed from Him. Creation—by which the world originates, and by which each soul originates—is spoken of as belonging especially to the Father.

Again, within the divine Nature, the Holy Spirit is Love, the utterance of the love of Father and Son. Sanctification, grace—these are gifts, and gifts are the work of love: they are appropriated to the Holy Spirit. Grace is a created gift of love; the Holy Spirit is the uncreated gift of love. By grace, Father and Son express their love for us— as eternally they express their love for each other—in the Holy Spirit.

Is there any similar appropriation to the Second Person? As we have noted, He is called Redeemer; but not by appropriation, since He did in fact redeem us Himself: it was not Father, Son and Holy Spirit who became man and died for us, but the Son only (Redemption was not an operation of the divine nature but of the human nature He made His own). But He has His appropriation all the same.

In the Creed, God the Father is called Creator, and we have just seen why. But in the opening of Saint John's Gospel, the Second Person seems to be Creator too. Creation, as a work of origination, bringing something into existence where nothing was, is appropriated to the Father. But what was brought into existence was not a chaos, but a universe ordered in its elements; it was a work of wisdom, therefore, and as such appropriated to the Second Person, the Word of God, who proceeds by the way of knowledge. The structure of the universe and all things in it, the order of the universe, is attributed especially to the Son; and when the order was brought to disorder by sin, it was the Son who became man to repair the disorder and make the new order of redeemed mankind.

But the perfect aptness of the attribution of operations to one or other Person must not blind us to the reality that in all these operations all three Persons are at work. Grace comes, says Our Lord, from the indwelling of the Holy Spirit in our souls; but He also says, "If anyone love Me, he will keep My word, and My Father will love him, and We will come to him and make our abode with him." So it is in fact an indwelling of all three Persons. Then why have appropriation at all?

In order, one may assume, to keep the distinction of the three Persons ever present to our minds. If we invariably spoke of every divine operation upon us as the work of God, or the work of the three Persons, we might come to feel that there was no real distinction between them at all, that Father, Son and Spirit were simply three ways of saying the same thing.

But appropriation is a constant reminder to us that they are distinct; not only that, it reminds us of the personal character of each—that the Father is Origin, the Son proceeds by the way of Knowledge, the Holy Spirit by the way of Love.

VI

THE HUMAN MIND AND THE DOCTRINE OF THE TRINITY

Mystery

The Trinity being the supreme mystery of our religion, this is a good moment to clarify our notion of mystery: which does not mean a truth that we cannot know anything about, but a truth that we cannot know everything about.

The first step is to see why it must be, and this happily does not call for any vast insight. The moment our mind has to cope with a mind superior to itself, the processes and the products of the superior mind must be largely shrouded in mystery to the lesser. We cannot see how the other mind arrives where it does, and we can comprehend only part of what it has arrived at. Nor do we see this as any reason for rejecting the other's insights. If we are sane, we are delighted that the world should contain greater minds than our own: it would be a poor prospect for the world if it did not: it would be a poor world in which your mind or mine was the best mind existent.

Given that God exists at all, it is clear that His ways are even less our ways than Einstein's or Shakespeare's, and that however much their minds may tower over ours, they still bear no proportion at all to infinite mind. A

Shakespeare wholly comprehensible by us would be not worth our reading; a wholly comprehensible God would be no God, and no use. Of the ocean of intellectual light which the mind of God is, we can receive but flashes and gleams, and immeasurably luminous they are in our poor darkness. But it would be a gross error to mistake them for the whole ocean, and a gross folly to wish that they were.

In studying God we begin with darkness, knowing nothing. We progress into light and revel in it, and at last we find ourselves face to face with darkness again, but a very different darkness from the first, a darkness richer than our light. It is the experience of all who have set themselves to a real study of divine revelation, that as the mind begins to take hold of the great realities proposed to it, they seem to be all light; and it is only as they come to live in the light that they are aware of the mightier darkness, which must be because God is infinite and we are not. The theologian sees far more "difficulties" in the doctrine of the Blessed Trinity than the beginner, and it would be strange if he did not. Nor does he repine at this, but rejoices. It was one of the greatest of theologians who created the phrase *caligo quaedam lux*— the darkness is a kind of light. It is a kind of light in two ways, a lesser and a greater; the lesser because it involves seeing why the mind can see no further: it is not merely baffled by mystery, but to that extent enlightened by it; the greater because of the very richness of the felt darkness—if the light that they can see be such, what must the darkness be which is light too bright for human eyes?

Mystery presents itself to us not only as something we cannot see because the light is too strong for our eyes, but also (and sometimes worryingly), as the appearance of contradiction in the things we do see.

As we come to grasp what God has taught us through His Church, we find certain elements at which our intellects cry a challenge, certain others which stir our feelings to something very much like revolt. We find the notion of eternal suffering so painful that we cannot reconcile it with a loving God; or we find the doctrine of human freedom impossible to reconcile with God's omniscience.

The answer, of course, is that all these elements are reconciled in the whole, and we do not see the whole. But we know that God is not only all-wise, but all-good. What He does and what He reveals is supreme truth and supreme love. In that confidence we can ask God for light to see *how* it is truth or love; but our trust is not diminished by one iota if our prayer for that extra gleam of light is not granted.

Making the Doctrine Our Own

A man with an idea in his head and love in his heart is one man, not three men. God, knowing and loving, is one God—even though the Idea produced by His knowledge is a person, and the inward utterance of His love is a person; for as we have seen, the Idea remains within the mind that thinks it, the Lovingness within the nature that loves.

This is the answer to the question with which we began our study of the doctrine of the Trinity. This is what God's life consists of: the infinite interflow of knowing and loving among three, who are one God.

Theology has formulated the doctrine as "three Persons in one Nature". As a formula it is a masterpiece, one of the mightiest products of the grace-aided intellect. But while it remains a formula there is not much light or nourishment in it: there are plenty of Christians for whom "three Natures in one Person" would have just as much, or just as little, meaning.

Even so slight a study of the Processions as we have been making should have lifted us out of that low state. The Church has far more to teach us about the doctrine than I set down here—more light, more of that darkness which comes of light too bright for us. But we have begun to see meanings in the terms.

We must try to bring them together in our minds, and contemplate them, not as a lot of bits and pieces—person, nature, procession, generation, spiration—but as they have their place in the totality of the revelation God has given us of Himself. The mind must live with the idea of the infinite spirit—spaceless, timeless—uttering His self-knowledge in a Son, Father and Son uttering Their mutual love as a Breath in which the whole of Their being is breathed.

I suppose that most people who have made an effort to hear what God is telling us about His innermost self have had much the same experience as I. The first time I heard a really competent lecture upon the Trinity, I followed it well enough, admired it, but made nothing very much of it. A year later I heard a second lecture, and this time I think I grasped all that the lecturer was saying; I was lost in admiration at the intellectual perfection of the doctrine's structure, and from that time on I could have told anyone else the doctrine as it had been told to me.

But in no sense was it alive in my mind; it was simply an intellectual possession, something I could visit when I felt like it and enjoy visiting, then put away again into the back of the mind. It was a year or two later that another series of lectures came my way, and the doctrine was at last alive. For most people something like that happens—first an intellectual response, then a vital response, till the doctrine possesses the mind, and the mind would be desolate without it.

It was at the Last Supper, as Saint John tells us, that Our Lord gathered together all those hints he had been giving of a plurality within the one God, and gave His apostles the fullest statement of the doctrine of the Trinity. Thus it was just before He died as man that He told us of the deathless life He lives within the Godhead. It was just before He laid down His human life for us that He laid open His divine life to us. Considering this, it seems incredible that anyone should ask what difference it makes to us whether God be three Persons or one, or ask what we gain by knowing. God made man pours out to men His innermost life secret, and there are those who in effect answer, "All this is very interesting no doubt, but it is only about You: What difference does it make to me?"

It is only "in effect" that any Christian could speak thus. Put into words it would be intolerable. The sufficient reason for giving our whole mind to the doctrine is that it is the truth about God. Nonetheless, before moving on from God to the world He created, there will be one brief effort to show something of what there is in the doctrine for us!

God Is Love

We of the laity have not given much attention to the doctrine of the Blessed Trinity. We have not, for the most part, met God's desire to be known with a desire to know Him. One strong reason is that we do not quite see what there is in the doctrine, spiritually, for us.

The difficulty here is in principle the same as with every organic experience. You cannot know what food will mean to you till you eat it, or the joy of marriage till you marry. So with our doctrine. Only by taking it to yourself and living with it can you find what there is in it for you.

Yet even to one who has not had the vital experience, some things can be said.

Thus we learn that God has an adequate object for His infinite loving power. It is wonderful for us that He loves us: but, as we have seen, it would be idle to pretend that we are an adequate object for infinite love—we can neither comprehend it nor respond to it, save in the most meager way. It is as though a man on a desert island had only a dog to love—he simply could not love with the fullness of love possible to a man. It is only in the interchange of love with an equal that love reaches its height. If God had none to love but His inferiors, it would be hard to believe that God is love. But God is not thus doomed to love without ever finding an adequate object. In Son and Holy Ghost infinite love is infinitely accepted and infinitely returned.

Again, knowledge of the three Persons enriches our awareness of what is meant by ourselves being made in God's image.

Man is not only a unit composed of matter and spirit, who is, by his spirit and its powers, made in the image of the Infinite Spirit. Man cannot be understood as a unit at all; he is a social being, linked organically with others, neither brought into being nor maintained in being save by others. Community is of his very essence. And now we know that there is community within the very being of God, so that by that too we are in His image. Contemplating God we learn the secret of community, wonderfully defined by Saint Augustine—a community is a multitude united by agreement about the things they love. We learn the truth expressed by Saint Thomas—where each one seeks his rights, there is chaos. For the secret of the divine community is infinite giving.

As one goes on letting the mind live with the doctrine, new things are constantly emerging to answer the question of what gain there is in it for us. But even if no such things emerged for our obvious and statable profit, it still remains that our principal reason for accepting it and clinging to it is that it is true, and it is true about God. Intellect is one of the great twin powers of the soul. Insofar as it remains unnourished, our personality lacks full development. The food of the intellect is truth, and this is the supreme truth about the supreme Being. Merely as truth, it would be a defect of human dignity to ignore it. Thinking that there is only one Person in God is incomparably worse than thinking that the earth is flat. People would find the latter piece of ignorance intolerable, quite apart from any practical difference that the earth's sphericality makes to us: it would be shameful not to know. But ignorance about the Supreme Being is worse poverty than ignorance about any of the lesser beings He has created of nothing. Of these greater truths, as of all truths, the rule remains that it is sufficient reason for acceptance that they are true. If there were no other profit, that is sufficient profit.

We cannot go on forever talking about the blessed Trinity. It will be one of the joys of heaven that we shall be under no pressure to move away to other topics. We must next begin to talk of the beings God has created. Meanwhile we may summarize. God *is* Trinity. The Trinity is not an extra, it is God. If men omit the doctrine of the Trinity, because they do not know it, they can still be talking about God. But, if knowing it, they omit it, how are they talking about God? How are they talking *to* God?

VII

CREATION

God needs no being other than Himself. He not only contains within Himself the sufficient reason for His own existence, but every other sufficiency. To His limitless perfection, nothing whatever is lacking; there is no need of His nature that some lesser being could supply; there is no luxury, even, that some lesser being could bring Him. In His own nature is all being, all perfection, all bliss.

Why then did He create a universe? There can be vast theological discussion here but it can be reduced, not too crudely, to the single statement that He knew we should like it. Creation brings Him no gain, but it brings us tremendous gain: it means that we are something instead of nothing, with all the possibilities of life and growth and happiness instead of the mere blankness of nonentity.

It is a new light upon the love of God that our gain could be a motive for His action. He knew that beings were possible who could enjoy existence, and He gave them existence. By existing they glorify Him—but who is the gainer by that? Not God, who needs nothing from any creature: only the creature, whose greatest glory is that he can glorify God.

All Things of Nothing

We use the word "create" for this conferring of existence. God made all things of nothing. Of what else could He make them? Not of Himself, for He is utterly simple: in Him there are no parts which He can break off and, so to speak, set up in business on their own. Not of Himself then: and beside Himself, apart from creation, there is nothing.

So He used no material in creating the universe. He made it wholly—that is indeed the definition of "create", to make a thing wholly, to make the whole of it, and only God can do it. A carpenter does not make the whole of a chair, the wood already exists; a poet does not make the whole of a poem, the words already exist. But God did make the whole of the universe; there was no existing material to make it of, and He could do it because there is no limit at all to His power—"He can send His call to that which has no being, as if it already was" (Rom 4:17).

For the Catholic all this may seem old stuff. He cannot remember when he first learned that God had made him of nothing. Neither indeed can I. But I can remember very well when I first realized what it meant.

I was speaking on a Catholic Evidence Guild platform in Hyde Park. I remarked for the hundredth time, or perhaps the thousandth, that God had made me of nothing. But this time I heard what I was saying, and the experience was utterly shattering. To *realize* that one is made of nothing gives a feeling of hardly being there at all, a feeling that one has no hold on existence and might vanish away.

And all this because I had paid no attention at all to the truth that follows upon our being made of nothing—namely, that God continues to hold us in existence.

God made us of nothing, but by the mere act of His will He made us into something. And the same will that brought us into existence is required to keep us in existence. Think hard about this, for in it is the primary truth about ourselves; without it we shall not know the first thing about ourselves—the *first* thing.

A carpenter makes a chair. He leaves it, and the chair continues to exist. Why? Because the material he made it of preserves the shape he has given it. In other words, when the maker of a thing leaves it, it is kept in existence by the material used in its making. If God, having made us, left us, we should be kept in existence by the material used in our making—namely nothing.

This is the truth about the universe as a whole and every part of it (including ourselves). Unless from moment to moment God held it in being, it would simply cease.

Whatever are the ultimate constituents of matter, God made them of nothing and sustains them in existence. The highest created spirit equally was made by God of nothing and without Him could not endure.

What it is made *of* does not account for any being's coming into existence or remaining in existence; everything depends at every instant upon the God it is made *by*. That is one reason for giving the whole power of our mind to knowing God.

Without God All Is Meaningless

God made us and all things of nothing. We may look, and feel, pretty substantial, so much flesh and blood and bone: but the matter of our body God made of nothing (as He made our soul); and it has nothing but what God has given it. God holds us and all things in being. As we have seen, if He withdrew His will for our existence, we should be nothing: I do not mean that we should die, I mean that we should be nothing at all.

Not to know these two truths is to be wrong about everything. If we omit God, we see nothing as it is but everything as it is not—which is the very definition of insanity.

God is the explanation of everything. Leave out God, then, and you leave out the explanation of everything, you have everything unexplainable. Science studies the constitution of matter—what things are made of. But no science can study the two far more vital questions—*by whom* were they made, for *what* were they made.

I have called these more vital, and so they are. Consider one thing only. You cannot use anything intelligently until you know what it is made for. Science cannot tell you what the universe was made for: only its Maker can do that—because He knows what He had in mind when He made it.

And it is not only the whole universe that we see wrong if we leave out God. We do not see any single thing right. God is at the center of the being of each individual thing, giving it the existence it has, keeping it in existence. To see anything—yourself, for instance—without in the same act seeing God holding it in existence is to be living in a world of fantasy, not the real world.

You see a coat hanging on a wall; with the eyes of your body you do not see the hook, because the hook is under the coat; but with the eyes of your mind you see the hook, all right. Supposing you did not: it would mean that you thought the coat was hanging on the wall by its own power: you would be wrong about the nature of coats, the nature of walls, the law of gravity. You would be living in wonderland. If the failure to see so small a thing as a hook means a deranged universe, how much more the failure to see God—on whom everything depends, including the hook.

God is not just a sublime extra. It is not that we see the same things as other people, plus God. Even the things we and they both see do not look the same, and in fact are not the same. Think of a physical landscape at sunrise; it is not that you see the same hills and trees and houses as before, and now you see the sun as well. The sun is not just one more item; you see everything sun-bathed. God is not just one more item; we must see everything God-bathed. Only then are we seeing everything as it is.

Of course it is not only a question of seeing; this truth effects our actions too. Sin, for instance, is an effort to gain something against the will of God; but the will of God is all that holds us in existence; when we sin, we are hacking away at our only support! What could be more idiotic? The realization may not prevent us from sinning; but it ensures that we shall feel fools while doing it. God's will is the only law for sane people.

Yet this concentration upon the nothing God *made us of* must not lead us to think that we *are* nothing. That would be an insult to our Maker. For if He made us of nothing, He made us into something. We are not just thoughts in His mind. We really exist. And that we are kept in existence only by the will of God does not mean that we have no secure hold on existence: we hold it so securely—or rather God holds us so securely in it—that it is the one thing we cannot be rid of; even death does no more than change the condition of our existence: we cannot cease.

Matter, Angels, Men

The universe God created has two vast divisions—spirit and matter. From the point of view of creation, the one difference between them is paramount. For while everything made by God bears the mark of its Maker, so that to the observant eye it points straight to Him and tells much of Him, spiritual beings alone are made in His image and likeness.

We have here something like the difference between an artist painting a picture—of a landscape, say, or a friend—and painting a self-portrait. The material universe is God's work of art, but spiritual beings are His self-portraiture. Our own soul is a spirit, so that every man bears a portrait of God, painted by God, within him. It is painted by God, for every soul is a new creation, made by God in His own image; but in most of us the likeness of God is sadly defaced by sin.

Man's soul, of course, as we have already seen, is not the highest of created spirits, it is the lowest. Over it tower the angels. They are pure spirits—that is, they have no bodily element at all—simply minds and wills, minds knowing, wills loving, both at an intensity of power beyond our conception.

That angels exist we know by God's revelation. Science, which has developed marvelous skill in the examination of matter, can make no pronouncement at all as to these beings in whom there is no faintest element of matter.

We call them angels—the word means messengers—because of so many instances in Scripture where God uses them to convey His will to men; but of course they do not exist for us, any more than we for them: we and they alike exist for God. Yet they *are* our mightier brothers and their love and their protection are ours for the asking. "What are they, all of them, but spirits apt for service, whom He sends out when the destined heirs of salvation have need of them?" (Heb 1:14). When Our Lord was in agony in Gethsemane, His Father sent an angel to comfort Him. We sometimes need comfort ourselves.

From end to end, Scripture is so filled with the activities of angels that it is puzzling to find so many Christian bodies ignoring them altogether, save as ornaments on Christmas cards. But even we who are Catholics overlook them very easily, to our great loss. We know from Our Lord's words that every child has an angel to guard him; and it is the universal teaching of theologians that this is so not only of children but of all: yet we seldom turn to them for help.

We tend to forget about angels simply because they *are* spirits. Matter is not so easy to overlook. Angels can nourish our minds, as cows our bodies; we are more solicitous for the nourishment cows give. Fallen angels can damage our souls, as microbes our bodies: we are more on our guard against microbes. Sanity demands that we correct this strange defect in our seeing.

The universe God called into being has in it these two great divisions—the world of spirits and the world of matter. It is the special reason for man's existence that he makes these two worlds, locks these two worlds, we might say, into one universe by belonging to both. Without man, spirit and matter would be two spheres, not touching; but man belonging to one by his soul, the other by his body, joins them together. Think of the universe, not as two unrelated spheres, but as a figure eight, with man on both sides of the join.

This is man's special function in the universe: his body is not just an accident, a punishment for sin from which he is to work free, a temporary embarrassment to be shed at death as a butterfly sheds its cocoon: it is essential if he is to act his part in the universe. That is one reason for the resurrection of our bodies at the Last Day: we should not be men without them, but only inadequate angels.

Remember what was said of soul and spirit in Chapter II. They are not two words for the same thing. Spirit is a partless, spaceless, immortal being, which can know and love. Soul means principle of life in a living body: man has the only soul that is a spirit, the only spirit that is a soul.

How God Created

The question of how God created falls naturally into two questions—what the creative act meant in terms of God whose act it was, and in terms of the universe which resulted from God's act.

As to the first question: God willed that things which were not should come to be. He simply willed it. He is omnipotent, limitless in power, and therefore He requires neither material to work upon nor any process of manufacture. His will is enough. The reader might profitably linger on two texts of Scripture. One is from the Psalms: "He spoke and they were made; He commanded and they were created" (148:5). The other is from Romans: "He can send His call to that which has no being as if it already was" (4:17).

By revelation we can go further. Creation was the work of the Blessed Trinity, the three Persons acting as one creator. Just as Father and Son produce the Holy Spirit, so Father, Son and Holy Spirit create the universe. Here we should reread what has been said of appropriation (pp. 46ff.). The Creeds speak of God the Father as Creator of heaven and earth. But Scripture is insistent, too, that all things were created by the Son (Jn 1:3, Heb 1:2).

We have seen how the two truths combine. That something should come into existence of nothing is a work of pure origination: as such, creation is "appropriated" to the Father, who within the Blessed Trinity is Origin. But the something that results is not just anything; it is an ordered something, ordered in itself and in its possibilities of development: as such it is a work of Wisdom and is "appropriated" to the Son, who is the uttered Wisdom of the Father. When the order was wrecked, it was the Son who became man to restore it.

The second of our two questions was what the creative act meant in terms of the universe: Had we been looking at the time, what should we have seen? Nobody, naturally, was looking. Of that first instant before which there was no instant, we can know only as much as God tells us. The telling is in the opening two chapters of the Bible's opening book, Genesis (which means "Beginning"). Please read them carefully: we shall be much occupied with them.

They tell of a creation of the world in six days; as we read on in the Old Testament, the surface meaning seems to be that it all happened roughly four thousand years before the birth of Christ. Scripture did not require the surface meaning, but having no reason to do otherwise, men generally did, up to a century ago, take the four thousand years for granted. Modern science—geology especially—provided reason against believing the four thousand years and they were dropped painlessly. Man is immeasurably older, and the universe immeasurably older still.

What of the six days? What of the order Genesis gives for the emergence of sun and moon and the rest? The Fathers and Doctors of the Church never thought of Genesis as giving us a scientific blueprint of creation. Around the end of the fourth century, over fourteen hundred years before Darwin, Saint Augustine wrote *De Genesi ad litteram*, establishing that Genesis was not meant to be taken literally. His own view was that in the beginning God created the "seeds", the elements which would ultimately develop, evolve, into our universe. (He has a couple of theories about the six days, neither of them literal.)

The burning question, of course, was as to the creation of man. Genesis speaks of two elements—earth and the breath of God. "The Lord God formed man of the slime of the earth" and "breathed into his face the breath of life; and the man became a living soul". Did the word "formed" mean one single, instantaneous action? Or could it mean a long process, animal bodies slowly developing (under God's guidance) until at last one was evolved capable of union with a spiritual soul? Obviously the word "formed" could mean either: of itself it does not tell us.

Nor does the Church. Catholics may, if they will, believe in an immediate creation of the human body from elements in the earth; they are allowed to believe in an evolutionary process by which the first human body comes from the earth by way of other animal bodies.

What they must not deny is the immediate creation, for the first man and every subsequent man, of the soul. The soul, being a spirit, having no parts, cannot evolve from some lower form; it can exist only if God creates it.

VIII

THE NATURE OF MAN

Soul and Body

Having reached this point, the Catholic reader is usually anxious to get on to the story of the Fall of Man. He feels that the Fall is the really interesting thing, Creation being only a necessary preliminary. There could be no Fall till Creation provided the man and the woman; but once the man and the woman have arrived, there's no need to linger: he wants to get on with the story: What, he feels, are we waiting for?

But we, who are studying theology, cannot go racing on like that. If we do, we shall simply not understand the Fall, or indeed anything else that has happened to man. We must linger on Creation to see two things principally. The first is what the being was who fell—that is we must look more closely at the nature of man. The second is what he fell from and why it mattered—that is we must study God's plan for the race He had created. Only then can we go on to see what man made of God's plan. It will be many pages yet before we come to the Fall.

Come back to the two elements in the creation of man. "The Lord God formed man of the slime of the earth"; that accounts for his body. And "He breathed into his face the breath of life." That may occupy us rather longer.

"Breath", remember, is the name of the Third Person of the Trinity, for the root meaning of the word *spirit* is breath. Put this together with another phrase from Genesis: "Let us make man to our image and likeness." What God breathed into man was His own image and likeness—a spiritual soul. It is by our soul—partless, spaceless, immortal, capable of knowledge and love—that we resemble God. It is an improbable combination—the slime of the earth, and the spirit that is in the likeness of God.

We are so used to the combination, for every one of us is a specimen of it, that we may not remark how extraordinary it is. The Church frowns on mixed marriages, but every one of us is the result of the most mixed of all marriages, the wedding of spirit and matter. In this we are unique; no other being is compound of spirit and matter as we are: angels are spirit, with no matter to complicate it; cats are matter, with no spirit to complicate it.

But what does the union of these two improbable partners *mean*? There is need for a volume here, or perhaps a library. We must be content with a quick look. Every living body—plant, animal, man—has a principle of life, that is, it has a constituent which accounts for its being alive. This is its soul. We are aware of its presence in the activities of the being while it is alive; we are even more aware of its absence, in the corruption which follows death.

The souls, the life-principles, of plants and animals produce no vital activities which rise above matter: they are marvelous enough, they animate the body; in plants they make possible movement and growth and reproduction, in animals some faint likeness of knowledge, some faint beginning of social life, as well.

But the soul of man not only animates the body, it has powers of its own, powers utterly outside the possibilities of matter. Here it would be well to glance back once more at Chapter II. The union of spirit and matter means that the human soul, by which our bodies are living bodies and function as living bodies, is what no other soul is, a spirit.

The union is such that the soul is in every part of the body: and this again needs a closer look. The soul, being a spirit, is not in space at all. How can it be in every part of a body which is so very definitely spread out in space? Do not try to form a picture of a soul exactly the same shape as the body but made of thinner stuff (transparent, perhaps); or of the body thinly buttered with soul, so that every bit of body has a bit of soul. The soul is not in space at all; it animates the body by superiority of energy. A spirit is where it acts; the soul is in every part of the body because no part of the body escapes its life-giving action.

There, then, stands man. His soul, because it *is* a soul, animates his body, as the soul of a lower animal animates its; but because man's soul is a spirit, it has the faculties of intellect and will by which it knows and loves as the animal's cannot. To man's intellect, objects are present not only as those individual objects seen, but as *what they are*; it can abstract their essence, analyze, generalize, reflect, build up all the great structures of thought, come to the knowledge of spirit and of the Infinite Spirit, grow in the domination of the material universe. We are proud of our dog when he brings in the morning paper; pleased with a chimpanzee which has been trained to smoke or drink from a cup; but animal knowledge is only a faint parody of human knowledge. And so, with all its pathos, is animal love.

This superiority of the spiritual soul spreads downward— to the border region between soul and body, to imagination and sense memory and the emotions, in none of which has the animal more than hints and suggestions of the human. It spreads to the body itself.

We have not space here to develop the final point in the relation of soul and body as the philosopher would; but at least remember that they are not two separate things, one of which animates the other; they are combined in one being, man himself. By its substantial union with a spiritual soul, man's body is—shall we say spiritualized?—not mere matter anyway, but ennobled. If, by some impossible chance, one of the lower animals were given a human body, he would not know what to do with it.

But even when we have seen man as a union of spirit and matter, we have not seen him whole and entire. Two other truths about him must be seen, or we see him wrong.

The first is that man is essentially a social being. We should not come into existence unless other humans produced us, or stay in existence unless they maintained us in it. This dependence on others we do not outgrow. We have all sorts of needs which we cannot supply for ourselves; and all sorts of powers—to love, for example, to teach, to procreate—which can never be used save in relation to others. Without his fellowman, no one would ever reach maturity; he would be a rough sketch for a man, no more.

God's Law and Freedom

The second is the truth we have already seen as applying to all beings whatever. Man is made by God of nothing, is held in existence from moment to moment simply by God's will to hold him there. God's will is the reason for man's existence; so God's will must be the law of his existence. To disobey the law is sin; to think we can gain by disobeying it is insanity.

That there are laws in the universe, no one doubts: the law of gravity is one obvious example: the laws of dietetics are another. By learning these laws and living according to them we gain freedom. Pause upon this, if the thought is new to you. Freedom is always bound up with obedience to the law of God; there is no such thing for man as freedom from these laws, there is only freedom within them. Each new law learned by us increases our freedom. We learn the laws of gravity, air currents, movement of bodies: and at last we can fly in the upper air. We learn what elements are necessary in our diet, and certain diseases vanish.

That there are laws applying to man's soul, moral laws, is just as true. The same God who made the law of gravity, made the laws of justice and purity. Physical laws do not affect only those who accept them—the newborn baby can die for want of the right vitamins or be killed by falling from a height. It is the same with the laws of morality. Because both sorts are laws, we cannot break them. How could we break the law of gravity? We could jump off a cliff, but by doing that we should not break the law of gravity, we should illustrate it.

We cannot break the laws, but, if we ignore them, they can break us. In this the laws of morality are the same as physical laws. If we disobey them, even in ignorance, our nature is always damaged, for they are the laws of reality. If we disobey them, knowing that God has commanded us to obey them, then there is sin, the worst damage of all.

The moral laws being of such importance to man, how does he know what they are? In two ways principally—by the witness of his nature, and by the teaching of men entitled to speak in the name of God.

Take nature first. God, making creatures, built the laws of their being into them. The maker of an automobile does much the same: he builds his machine to run with water in the radiator, with gasoline in the tank, with a proper order in the gears; that way it will function. God makes our bodies, with lungs that need air and with a complex mechanism to ensure that they get it, with a need for certain kinds of food, and so on. By powers, and by felt needs that will cause us to exercise the powers, God builds His laws into our body; in obedience to them, the body is in health.

In the same way, God builds His laws into our souls, too. The laws of justice and purity and worship are as real for the soul as the laws of diet for the body. In obedience to them, the soul is in health.

If we disobey the laws for the running of the automobile, the engine makes strange noises and at last comes to a stop. If we disobey the laws of the body, we have pain, and ultimately death. The stirring of conscience in the soul is like the strange noises in the engine and the pain in the body; it is a protest against misuse. It is the soul's way of indicating that the laws according to which its Maker built it are being ignored, that it is not being run as its Maker built it to be run.

This pain in the soul is unlike any other—it is an intense awareness that we *ought not* to be acting as we are, that a particular action is not merely damaging us but is wrong. Even if the action is apparently pleasurable and profitable— as when one takes another man's money or wife—there is this inner protest to spoil the pleasure and make the profit questionable.

This inner protest is not by itself a sufficient guide; we are no longer as God made us; the generations have introduced distortions at this point or that, habits and ideas have taken root and grown into a second nature, silencing nature's first utterance. For any given man or society, the inner witness sounds surely on most matters; but there are those on which it does not sound. For certainty, we need the statement of God's appointed teachers.

Conscience is the practical moral judgment of the intellect, the intellect's judgment upon the rightness and wrongness of our own actions. The intellect makes its judgment according to God's law known to it in one or other of the two ways we have been discussing.

As only God can tell us with certainty the laws by which we should live, so only God can tell us with certainty the purpose of our life. We cannot use anything intelligently until we know what it is for. Men apply the rule as a matter of course to everything—to everything, that is, except one thing: themselves. Yet, it is no less clear about man himself than about all other things. We cannot intelligently handle our own lives, or influence the lives of others, unless we know what man is for.

There is no space to develop this idea here, but please reflect on it. Unless we know the goal man is meant to reach, we cannot direct our own life toward it or help others to reach it. To walk the road of life, not knowing where it leads to, is mere blindness.

Our Maker has told us what He made us for—to come to the fullest development of our own powers in total union with Him.

Let us take a first look at this. Man's highest powers are intellect, by which he knows, and will, by which he loves (and, according to his love, chooses). The object of the intellect is truth, of the will goodness. Our intellect is to come to the fullest knowledge of the supreme truth— which is God. Our will is to come to the fullest love of the supreme goodness—which is God.

In knowing and loving God we shall achieve the purpose for which God made us. So much we might have guessed without any revelation from God. What we could never have suspected, without His telling, is what the knowing and loving are to be.

IX

THE SUPERNATURAL LIFE

A Goal above Our Nature

"Eye has not seen nor has ear heard, nor has it entered into the heart of man, what things God has prepared for those who love Him." So Saint Paul tells the Corinthians, quoting Isaiah. Until we reach heaven, we shall not know what heaven is. But, in the inspired word of God, we are given glimpses. In heaven we shall know God in a new way, and love Him according to the new knowledge.

We shall know, says Saint Paul (1 Cor 13:12), as we are known. It is a mysterious phrase, more dark than light, but soliciting our minds powerfully. We are not to know God with the same knowledge with which He knows us—for He knows infinitely and we are incurably finite, but with a knowledge similar in kind to His, different from our present way of knowing.

In the same verse, Saint Paul makes another attempt to express the difference between our knowing here and our knowing there. "Here we see through a glass in a dark manner, but then face to face." Saint John (1 Jn 3:2) says, "We shall see Him as He is." And we remember Our Lord saying of the angels (Mt 18:10), "They see the face of my heavenly Father continually." Seeing is the key to life in heaven.

We can approach the meaning in two steps. First, those in heaven shall *see* God, not simply believe in Him as now but *see* Him. Here on earth we do not say that we believe in the existence of our friends, we see them; and seeing them, we know them. But, second, we shall see God face to face, see Him as He sees us.

The Church has worked out for us a first beginning of the meaning of this. Concentrate upon the way we know our friends. Our knowing faculty, our intellect, has taken them into itself. How? By the idea it has formed of them. By means of that idea, we know *them*. The richer the idea, the better we know them; if there is any error in our idea of them, to that extent we do not know them as they are. This is the way of human knowledge, the "seeing through a glass in a dark manner" which is the kind of seeing proper to human nature. It is the nature of our intellect to know things by means of the ideas it forms of them.

Here below we know God like that, by the idea we have formed of Him. But in heaven, our seeing will be *direct*. We shall see Him, not "through a glass", we shall know Him, not by means of an idea. Our intellect will be in direct contact with God; nothing will come between it and God, not even an idea. The nearest we can get to it, perhaps, is to think of the idea we now have of God: then try to conceive of God Himself taking the place of the idea.

That is why the very essence of the life of heaven is called the Beatific Vision—which means the seeing that causes bliss.

Just as our knowing faculty, the intellect, so our loving faculty, the will, is to be in direct contact with God, nothing coming between, God in the will, the will in God, love without detour or admixture. So it will be with every one of our powers—energizing at its very fullest upon its supreme object. And that, if you will think about it, is the definition of happiness.

But observe that all this is based upon doing something which by nature we cannot do. The natural powers of man's intellect fall short of seeing God directly by a double limitation: as we have seen, our natural way of knowing is always by means of ideas, so that we cannot see anything directly; and God, being infinite, can never be within the hold of our natural strength, or the strength of any finite being whatever.

Putting it bluntly, the life of heaven requires powers which by nature we do not possess. If we are to live it, we must be given new powers. To make a rough comparison: if we wanted to live on another planet, we should need new breathing powers, which by nature our lungs have not got. To live the life of heaven, we need new knowing and loving powers, which by nature our souls have not got.

For heaven our natural life is not sufficient; we need supernatural life. We have it only by God's free gift, which is why we call it grace (the word is related to *gratis*). Sanctifying grace will be our next topic. Everything the Church does is connected with it and can be understood but cloudily if we do not grasp what it is.

Sanctifying Grace

When we come to die there is only one question that matters—have we sanctifying grace in our souls? If we have, then to heaven we shall go. There may be certain matters to be cleared, or cleansed, on the way, but to heaven we shall go, for we have the power to live there. If we have not, then to heaven we cannot go; not because we lack the price of admission, but because quite simply our soul lacks the powers that living in heaven calls for.

It is not a question of getting past the gate, but of living once we are there; there would be no advantage in finding a kindly gatekeeper, willing to let us in anyhow! The powers of intellect and will that go with our natural life are not sufficient: heaven calls for powers of knowing and loving higher than our nature of itself has. We need super-natural life, and we must get it here upon earth. To die lacking it means eternal failure.

We must look at grace more closely if we are to live our lives intelligently.

Two things about it must be grasped.

First: It *is* supernatural, it is wholly above our nature, there is not even the tiniest seed of it in our nature capable of growing, there is nothing we can do to give it to ourselves. We can have it only as God gives it, and He is entirely free in the giving. That, as we have seen, is why it is called grace; and because its object is to unite us with God, it is called sanctifying grace.

Second: Even the word *supernatural* does not convey how great a thing it is. It is not simply above our nature, or any created nature. It enables us to do—at our own finite level, but really—something which only God Himself can do by nature: it enables us to see God directly. That is why it is called "a created share in the life of God". That is why those who have it are called "sons of God": a son is like in nature to his father; by this gift we have a totally new likeness to Our Father in heaven.

Giving us this new life, God does not give us a new soul with new faculties. He inserts it, sets it functioning, in the soul we already have. By it our intellect, which exists to know truth, is given the power to know in a new way; our will, which exists to love goodness, is given the power to love in a new way.

We get the supernatural life here on earth. Not until we reach heaven will it enable us to see God face to face and love Him in the direct contact of the will. But even on earth its elevating work has begun; it gives the intellect a new power of taking hold of truth—by faith; it gives the will new powers of reaching out to goodness—by hope and by charity.

Faith, then, does not mean simply feeling that we believe more than we used to; hope does not mean simply feeling optimistic about our chances of salvation; charity does not mean simply feeling pleased with God. All three may have their effect on our feelings; but they are not feelings; they are wholly real.

The supernatural life in our souls is a new *fact*, as real as the natural life we have to start with. The powers it gives are facts too; they enable us to do things which without them we could not do: they are as real as eyesight, and considerably more important. Without eyesight, we could not see the material world. But without sanctifying grace we should not be able to see God directly, which is the very essence of living in heaven.

Not only that: here below we should not be sharers of the divine life, sons of God, capable already of taking hold of God by faith and hope and charity, capable of meriting increase of life. This increase of life must be realized; one can be more alive or less, and our life in heaven will differ according to the intensity of faith and hope and charity in our souls when we come to die.

We shall go on to consider these three virtues in detail. Meanwhile concentrate upon one truth: grace is not just a way of saying that a soul is in God's favor; it is a real life, with its own proper powers, living in the soul; and he who has it is a new man.

A soul with sanctifying grace in it is indwelt by God. Here the reader may raise a question. Since every created thing has God at the very center of its being, maintaining it in existence, surely all things whatsoever are indwelt by God: in what can God's indwelling the soul by grace differ from that?

That first presence of God by which we exist is not called indwelling: for this word means God making Himself at home in the soul, and it is not merely fanciful to think that this can only be by invitation. About the first presence we have no choice: we did not invite God to bring us into being, and it is not because we ask Him that He keeps us in being. The choice is wholly His. No request of ours would move Him to withdraw His presence: in the depths of hell He is there, maintaining each spirit in existence. It is a fearful thing to have nothing of God but His presence, to have existence from Him and nothing more, refusing all the other gifts that the creature needs and only God can give.

But the indwelling *is* by invitation. If we receive sanctifying grace in infancy, the sponsor extends the invitation on our behalf; as we come to the use of reason, we make the invitation our own. At any time we can withdraw it, and God's indwelling ceases, leaving us only His presence. The God who indwells is the Blessed Trinity. Father and Son and Holy Spirit make the soul their home, acting upon the soul, energizing within it, while it reacts to their life-giving, light-giving, love-giving energy. That essentially is the process of sanctifying grace.

Faith, Hope, Charity

By sanctifying grace the soul has new powers—the theological virtues of faith, hope and charity; the moral virtues of prudence, justice, temperance and fortitude; the gifts of the Holy Spirit. We shall here speak only of the first three.

They are called "theological" because they have God not only for their end but for their object. It is worth our while to pause upon the distinction. All our actions should have God for their end or goal; that is, they should be aimed to do His will, to praise Him and thank Him and bring us closer to Him. But they cannot all have God for their object. The organist plays for the glory of God, and the cook bakes a cake for the love of God; God is the end of their action. But He is not the object. The object of the one is the organ, of the other the cake; the organist who makes God and not the organ the object of his playing will produce strange noises; the cook who makes God and not the cake the object of her action will produce an inedible mess; neither will glorify God.

The moral virtues have God for their end, but for their object they have created things—how we shall best use these to bring us to God. But for the theological virtues, God is object as well as end. By faith we believe in God, by hope we strive toward God, by charity we love God.

God is their object. God is also in a special sense their cause. They are wholly from Him. By faith we have a new power in the intellect, enabling us to accept whatever God reveals simply because He reveals it. We may see it as mysterious; we may feel that it is beyond us; we may not see how to fit it either with some other of His revealed truths or with our own experience of life. But we do not doubt that what He says is so. By faith the soul accepts Him as the source of truth. And it does so, not by its own power but His. He gives the power, not our own reasoning; He sustains faith in us. Our hold upon anything we have arrived at for ourselves can never be surer than the mental process by which we got to it. Our faith rests upon God who initiates and sustains it.

Faith is the root of the whole supernatural life. With it come hope and charity and the rest. The soul is alive with them. To its own natural life of intellect and will, there is now added this new and higher life. The new life, like the old, is actually *in* the soul, as the power of sight is in the eye. And it never leaves the soul unless we withdraw the invitation.

Next we shall look more closely at hope and charity, with a glance at sin, by which the invitation is withdrawn.

Faith is directed to God as supremely truthful, hope to God as supremely desirable, charity to God as supremely good. Faith we have already glanced at; it is the simple acceptance of God as our teacher.

Hope is more complex. There are three elements in it: it desires final union with God, sees this as difficult, sees it as attainable. The nature of hope comes out more clearly as we see the two ways of sinning against it, by presumption and by despair. *Despair* will not believe in the *attainability*, the sinner seeing himself as beyond the reach of God's power to save. *Presumption* ignores the *difficulty*, either by assuming that no effort on our part is necessary since God will save us whatever we do, or by assuming that no aid from God is necessary since our own effort can save us unaided. The answer to both is Saint Paul's "I can do all things in Him that strengthens me."

Charity is simple again. It is love of God. As a necessary consequence it is love of all that God loves; it is love of every image or trace or reflection of God it finds in any creature. Whatever the soul in charity loves, it loves for what of God is in it, the amount of God's goodness it expresses or mirrors. This is true love, since it means loving things or persons not for what we can get out of them but for what God has put into them, not for what they can do for us but for what is real in them. It means loving things or persons for what they are, and it is rooted in loving God for what He is. (This we have already noted is the strongest reason for *learning* what He is—that is, for studying theology.)

Supernatural Habits

Faith, hope and charity are called *habits* by the theologians, and this is not simply a technicality. If we think over our natural habits, we see that there is a real change in ourselves after we acquire them, something in our very natures leading us to act in certain ways—to drink cocktails, for instance, or answer back sarcastically. We say that a given habit grows on us. Really it grows *in* us, becomes second nature. The theologians apply the word to any modification, whether in body or soul, which disposes us either to do things we did not do before or do more easily or competently things we did. The skill of a pianist is a habit.

It is in this sense that the theological virtues are habits. They are really *in* our very souls, and they enable us to do things which without them would be impossible for us. They differ from natural habits in the way we acquire them. A natural habit is acquired gradually, as we repeat some particular action over and over again: supernatural habits are given to us in an instant by God. They differ again in the way they are lost. To be rid of a natural habit—drinking cocktails again—we must make a long series of efforts; supernatural habits are lost by one mortal sin against them. But while we have them, habits they are, in the meaning just given.

The drama of the Christian life is that, in acquiring the supernatural habits, we do not lose the natural habits. Our soul has the supernatural power to act toward God, but it has a natural habit of acting for self, ignoring God. It has the supernatural ability to make the unseen its goal, but a natural habit of being overwhelmed by the attractions of the visible. By steadily acting upon such natural habits as run counter to the supernatural we may, with our own efforts and God's grace, bring our nature and its habits wholly into harmony with supernature and the habits that belong to it.

For all of us it is a lifelong struggle. And its scene is the will. The will is that in us which *decides*, and it decides according to what it loves. In obedience to God, our will is the point of contact through which the supernatural life flows to us. A mortal sin—a serious and deliberate choice of our own will as against God's—breaks the contact, we lose the virtue of charity, supernaturally we are dead. We may still have the habits of faith and hope, which can be lost only by sins directly against them; but they are no longer life-giving. Only charity makes the soul and its habits come alive. That is why "the greatest of these is charity." (Now read 1 Corinthians, Chapter 13.)

X

THE FALL

Fall of Angels

All spiritual beings, angels and men alike, are created by God with the Beatific Vision, the direct vision of Himself, as their destiny. All of them need supernatural life to give them the powers of seeing and loving that their destiny calls for. And for all there is an interval—for growth or testing—between the granting of supernatural life and its flowering in the Beatific Vision. Once God is seen as He is, with the intellect in the immediate contact of sight and the will in the immediate contact of love, it is impossible for the soul to see the choice of self against God as anything but repulsive, and in the profoundest sense meaningless; in the immediate contact, the self knows beatitude, total well-being, and no element in the self could even conceive of wishing to lose it. But until then, the will, even supernaturally alive, may still choose self.

So it was with the angels. God created them with their natural life, pure spirits knowing and loving, and with supernatural life. And some of them chose self, self as against God. We know that one was their leader; him we call the Devil, the rest demons; he is the named one—Lucifer (though he is never called so in Scripture), Satan which means Enemy, Apollyon which means Exterminator,

Beelzebub which means the Lord of Flies. The rest are an evil, anonymous multitude.

The detail of their sin we do not know. In some form it was, like all sin, a refusal of love, a turning of the will from God, who is supreme goodness, toward self. Theologians are almost at one in thinking it was a sin of pride; all sins involve following one's own desire in place of God's will, but pride goes all the way, putting oneself in God's place, making oneself the center of the universe. It is total folly of course, and the angels knew it. But the awareness of folly does not keep us from sinning and did not keep them. The world well lost for love—that can be the cry of self-love too. One of the secondary theological excitements of the next life will be learning the detail of the angels' sin.

The angels who stayed firm in the love of God were admitted to the Beatific Vision. The rest got what they had asked for—separation from God: He still maintained them in existence out of their original nothingness, but that was all. Note that their choice was final. Men are given another chance, and another, and another. Not so angels. We have no experience, and never shall have it, of being pure spirits, spirits not meant for union with a body as our souls are: but philosophers who have gone deep into the concept see reasons why an angel's decision can only be final, and a second chance therefore pointless.

The angels who sinned were separated from God. They must have known that this would mean suffering. God had made them, as He has made us, for union with Himself. Their nature, like ours, is a great mass of needs, needs which only God can meet. All spiritual beings need God, as (and immeasurably more than) the body needs food and drink and air. Deprived of these the body knows torment, and at last dies. Deprived of God a spirit knows torment, and cannot die. It is deprived of God by its own will to reject God, but that it will not change: its self-love is too monstrous. The lost will not have God, who alone can meet their needs, but who by the greatness of His glory shows their own self for the poor thing it is. Union with Him would be self-love's crucifixion, and self-love has become their all.

There is more to be said of hell than that, and later more will be said; but that is the essence of it. One single detail must be added. Hell is not simply a place of self-inflicted torment, it is a place of hate. Love, like all good things, has its source in God. Cut off from its source, it withers and dies. It is as though the moon, in love with its own light, rejected the sun. Hell is all hate: hate of God, hate of one another, hate of all the creatures of God, above all of those creatures who are made in the hated image.

Fall of Adam

God created man with the natural life of soul and body, and with sanctifying grace, God dwelling in his soul and pouring supernatural life into it. In addition He gave man preternatural gifts, not supernatural but rather perfections of the natural—guarding it against destruction or damage. Notable among these were immunity from suffering and death, and integrity. This last is perhaps the one we look back to with the greatest longing, for it means that man's nature was wholly at peace: the body was subject to the soul, the lower powers of the soul to the higher, the natural habits wholly harmonious with the supernatural, the whole man united with God.

The point of union, for the first man as for all spiritual beings, was in the will, the faculty which loves, which decides. And he willed to break the union. He sinned, disobeying a command of God. The detail of the sin we do not know—Genesis describes it as the eating of forbidden fruit, but we are not bound to see this as literal. Two things about it we do know.

Man fell by the tempting of Satan; it was the first engagement in a war which has gone on ever since and which will not end until the world ends.

And what Satan tempted our first parents with was the promise that, if they disobeyed, they should be like gods. Satan must have felt the full irony of it. Pride had wrecked him, pride should wreck men.

For Adam, the individual man, the results can be simply stated and simply comprehended. He had broken the union with God, and the life ceased to flow. He lost sanctifying grace; supernaturally he was dead.

He lost the preternatural gifts too. He could now suffer, he had come under the natural law of death; worst of all he had lost integrity, the subordination of lower powers to higher, in the rejection of his own subordination to God. From now on every element in him would be making for its own immediate and separate gratification: the civil war within man had begun.

For Adam, the man, the future could be as simply stated. He could repent, turning to God again; God would remake the contact and sanctifying grace would be in him once more. But the man it was in was a very different man. The preternatural gifts were not restored, so that integrity was not there: it was to a man with his powers warring among themselves and tugging away from God as often as not, that grace was given back. To figure his condition, we have but to look at ourselves.

But Adam was not only a man. He was *the* man. He was the representative man. For the angels the testing had been individual; each angel who fell did so by his own decision. But the human race was tested and fell in one man, the representative man. In his catastrophe every man till the end of time was involved. There has been much mockery about this, of the "Eve-ate-the-apple-we-get-the-stomach-ache" variety. But, with no disposition to mock, we can still find something baffling in it.

The difference between the testing of men and angels is not the problem. The angelic race could not be tested in an individual angel, for there is no angelic race. Men are related to one another, because we are all brought into being, procreated, by others. Not so angels. Each is created whole and entire by God; he can call no other angel father. Our souls are the direct creation of God, but by bodily descent we are all children of Adam. And in our father we fell. But why? How could his sin involve us? That is the real problem, and we must be grateful for any lights we can get upon it.

Obviously there is something in the solidarity of the whole human race clear to God but not to us, that He could so treat the race as one thing. Some involvement in the fate of others we take for granted—a father makes decisions for his family, a ruler for his people: the solidarity of the family and the nation sufficiently explains the fact of one man's will being decisive for all. We do not see a similar solidarity for all men whatsoever—the foreigner is remote from our mind, the dead more remote, the unborn remotest of all. But no one of them is remote to the eye of God, who not only makes all men, but makes them in His own image. God sees the whole race, every member of which He created, as one thing—somewhat as we see a family as one thing or even a man. The mere number and variety—myriads upon myriads of men—and the uncountable ages, do not impede the vision of the Eternal and Omniscient God.

Results of Adam's Fall

So all men were involved in the catastrophe of Adam's sin. We are all born with natural life only, without the supernatural life of sanctifying grace. That was the chief thing Adam lost for each of his descendants.

A certain precision is necessary here. We sometimes slip into thinking that if he had not sinned he would have kept grace and we could have inherited it from him. But grace is in the soul, and we do not inherit our souls; each soul is a new creation. Adam's obedience was the *condition* on which we should all have come into existence with grace as well as nature. He disobeyed, the condition was not kept, we are born without sanctifying grace.

That is what is meant by being born in original sin, which is not to be thought of as a stain on the soul, but as the absence of that grace without which we cannot, as we have seen, reach the goal for which God destined men. We may be given grace later but we enter life without it, with nature only.

And our nature too is not as Adam's was before he failed the condition, but as it was after. The gift of integrity, guaranteeing the harmony of man's natural powers, has gone. Each of our powers seeks its own outlet, each of our needs its own immediate gratification; we have not the subordination of all our powers to reason and of reason to God which would unify all our striving; every one of us is a civil war.

At two points principally the disorder is at its worst, the passions and the imagination.

Passions are good things given for man's service; but in our actual state they dominate us as often as they serve us—more often indeed, unless we make an effort at control which costs us appallingly. They were meant to be instruments which we should use: instruments should be in our grip; only too often we feel as if we were in theirs.

The imagination is a good thing, too. It is the picture-making power by which we can mentally reproduce sights seen, sounds heard, textures touched, tastes, scents. For the intellect, the knowing power, it is a necessary servant. Made as we are we could not very well live in a material universe without it. But all too often it is a master, substituting its pictures for the hard effort the intellect should be making, refusing to let the intellect accept spiritual truths simply because imagination cannot make pictures of them.

It is worth our while to pause here and think over this dominance of imagination in ourselves—the times when we meant to think some problem out and imagination so distracted us that at the end of an hour we realized no thinking had been done; the times when we made some good resolution, and the mental picture of a girl or a drink shattered the resolution in an instant. And all because in Adam we lost the gift of integrity.

But it is not only as individuals that we were all involved in the catastrophe; we were involved as a race too. In Adam the race was tested. Before his sin the race—in him—was united with God; after, the unity was broken. There had been unity between the race and God; now there was a breach between them. Remember that, for God, the race is a fact, a reality. Each man is not only himself, he is a member of the race.

Because Adam broke the unity, his children were born members of a fallen race, a race no longer at one with God—a race, therefore, to which heaven was closed. A given man might be virtuous; but he was a virtuous member of a fallen race. Loving God, he might gain sanctifying grace, which means the power to live the life of heaven, but he still belonged to a race to which heaven was closed.

Only if the breach between his race and God could be healed, could he attain his own destiny, reach heaven; even naturally we are members one of another.

This is *the* problem created by the sin of the representative man. The race had been at one with God; it was no longer at one; the central problem was at-one-ment, a word whose meaning we disguise by pronouncing it atonement. With at-one-ment all the rest of our theology is concerned.

How to Restore a Fallen Race?

There has been an immense amount of theological thinking on atonement, at-one-ment, as a problem; more particularly as a problem the human race had set God. The sin of the race stood, and must remain forever an obstacle between men and their true destiny, unless either humanity could find some way of expiating it, making compensation for it, or God simply forgave it. Even with the sin expiated or written off, the breach remained and must remain unless God chose to remake the broken contact—not simply between individuals and Himself but between their race and Himself.

Fathers and Doctors of the Church have thought magnificently on what God could and could not do, on why the way He chose was the best way and whether it was the only way. But both the space at our disposal and our status as beginners in theology mean that this discussion is not for us—not here, not yet. We shall concern ourselves with atonement not as a problem but as a reality, not what God might have done but what He did.

We know that He meant to redeem mankind and heal the breach and make heaven once more open to men.

Because that was God's intention, He went on giving sanctifying grace to those who loved Him, a gift carrying with it the power to live in heaven and meaningless if heaven were never to be open to them.

We know that He meant to redeem. We may hope that our first parents knew it too. But the first statement of what He would do was strange; it did not carry its meaning on the surface; and it was addressed not to them but to Satan—the seed of the woman should crush his head.

Satan, in the shape of a serpent as Genesis relates, had tempted men to their ruin. They were to be punished; so was he. And Genesis shows God as ironically phrasing his punishment in terms of the serpent form Satan had adopted—he should go on his belly and eat the dust of the earth forever. He would continue to tempt man and one day man would defeat him utterly; these prophecies too were cast in serpent terms—Satan should lie in wait for man's heel, a descendant of the woman would crush his head.

I have lingered thus upon Satan because we so easily forget him. Even those who accept his existence forget his active malevolence, at most think of him as a sort of ugly extra, not a principal in the struggle of man's soul.

Our Lord did not see him as negligible. He called Him "a murderer from the beginning, a liar and the father of lies". As His own Passion and death were approaching, He spoke of Satan again and again. Here, in the very dawn, with the first human order wrecked, God's first statement of what He should do is made to Satan and in terms of Satan's overthrow.

What God would do, He would not do quickly. The disease admitted into humanity by the choice of self as against God was given every chance to run its course, work out its logic. God's providence did not desert man; those who implored Him were not left unaided; but it was

Satan's carnival all the same; he had gained no rights by his success over Adam, but he had gained immense power: he was the prince this world obeyed.

How long this first stage lasted we do not know, but as history at last begins to see mankind, the sight is at once heartening and horrifying: religion universal, everywhere twisted and tainted with lesser or greater perversions, but God never wholly forgotten and often marvelously remembered.

Four thousand years ago, the plan of redemption suddenly seems to take shape—at least to our eyes. God spoke to Abraham: his children were to be God's chosen people. Out of the chaos of the nations, one nation was to bear mankind's hopes. They were to be the guardians of monotheism, proclaiming that God is one; and of them was to be born the Savior of the world, the Messiah, the Anointed One. Of His Kingdom there should be no end.

The Jewish prophets multiplied their utterance upon both points—upon the one God and upon Messiah—with mixed success. By the time Messiah was due to come, indeed for centuries before, the Jews were unshakably monotheistic. But only rare ones among them had grasped the essential nature of the Kingdom the Savior was to found, and the supreme truth about the Savior Himself they did not know.

XI

THE REDEEMER

God Became Man

The supreme truth about the Savior, for which the Chosen People were wholly unprepared, was that He was God. To effect the redemption of the world, God became man. The inner meaning of God's plan, what made it redemptive, we shall not discuss yet. When we have seen what He did, we shall be in a position to grasp how it met the situation created by Adam's first sin, and worsened by all the sins with which men hastened to follow Adam's. We must concentrate our attention upon what actually happened.

God became man. Not the Trinity, but the Second Person of the Trinity, the Son, the Word, became man. Reread the opening verses of Saint John's Gospel. "The Word was with God, and the Word was God. All things were made by Him.... And the Word was made flesh, and dwelt among us." Here we find the fact—that it was the Second Person who became man. And we find the reason—"all things were made by Him."

Glance back at page 46, where appropriation is discussed. Creation as a work of omnipotence, bringing something into existence of nothing, is appropriated to God the Father. But the order of the universe, as a work of wisdom, is appropriated to the Son. The order had been wrecked, and a new order must be made; it was the Son who made it.

To make it, He became man. Read the first chapter of Saint Matthew and the first two of Saint Luke. A virgin, Mary, conceived a son; at the time she was betrothed, and soon after was married, to Joseph, a carpenter. The child thus conceived was God the Son. The Second Person of the Trinity, already and eternally existent in His own divine nature, now took human nature in Mary's womb.

His conception was virginal; He had a human mother but no human father; that which in ordinary conception is produced by the action of the father was in this instance produced by a miracle of the power of God. He grew in the womb like any other child, and in due course was born into our world in Bethlehem, near Jerusalem. He was named Jesus, and came to be called the Christ, which means the Anointed.

Of the next thirty years of His life we know little. He was a carpenter, in Nazareth, further north in Galilee. Then came the three years of His public life. He traveled over Palestine with the twelve followers He had chosen, the apostles. He preached of God and man, of the Kingdom, and of Himself as its founder; by every kind of miracle, of healing especially, He showed that God was guaranteeing the truth of His utterance. He was without mercy for the sinfulness of the religious leaders of the Jewish people. They could only want His death, and He gave them the pretext on which, in the name of true religion, they might kill Him. For He claimed to be, not Messiah only, but God.

Upon a charge of blasphemy, they persuaded the Roman governor of Judea to crucify Him.

He was nailed to a cross on a hill called Calvary for three hours until He died. He was buried, and on the third day He rose again. For forty days more He appeared among His apostles, then ascended into the sky until a cloud hid Him from their gaze. In His death, Resurrection and Ascension mankind is redeemed.

That is the story of our redemption in its barest outline. We must try to see its meaning, or as much of its meaning as is graspable this side of death.

The first step is to pierce as deep as we may into the being of Christ Our Lord. And for this we must read the Gospels. The newcomer to theology, even if he is not a newcomer to Gospel reading, should at this point in his study do what G. K. Chesterton advised—he should embark upon a reading of the Gospels *as though he had never read them before*, almost indeed as though he had never heard the story before. He must make the considerable effort to read what is there.

Two things especially make it difficult for us to read what is there.

The first is the extreme brevity of the four accounts. They are intensely concentrated, packed with meaning. We must learn to read them slowly, comparing one part with another, trying to *see* what they narrate or describe, living them as we read them.

The second is that we think we know it already. This can be a real obstacle to our hearing what the Gospels are actually saying. We flip through the first and second chapter of Saint Luke with a vague memory of Christmas cribs, Christmas carols, and Christmas cards. We move as inattentively through the four accounts of the Passion and death of Our Lord with the feeling that we have been through it all a thousand times in the Sorrowful Mysteries of the Rosary.

Above all we bring to the reading the popular picture of Our Lord as a nice kind man, easily pushed around, always turning the other cheek, happiest when patting small children's heads. So strong a grip has this imaginary portrait that it can prevent us meeting the strong and complex Christ who is actually there.

Our Lord as We Meet Him

We must read, then, with the determination to meet Our Lord, for ourselves, as He is. A reader coming wholly new to the story, not even thinking he had heard it before, would certainly become aware, after a while, of what I may call *a double stream* both of word and action. At times Our Lord is speaking and acting simply as man—a great man, an extraordinary man, but not more than a man. But at other times He says things and does things that go beyond the human: what He says and does is either a claim to be superhuman, or is utterly meaningless. Nor will the word "superhuman" long suffice. He says things that only God could say, does things that only God could do.

I shall not attempt to illustrate this double stream in detail. To get real value from the experience, each one should live through it for himself in the Gospels. In a way he will be living through the anguished questioning of the apostles in the three years they were with Him. At one moment they felt He must be more than man; then the feeling would fade only to return stronger, and perhaps fade again, but always revive.

Our Lord does not tell them at the beginning. The truth that the carpenter with whom they now lived so familiarly, whom they saw hungry and thirsty and weary, was the God by whom all things were made, was not one to be tossed casually to them or hurled violently at them. These men truly believed in God, had God's infinite majesty as the very background of all their lives. They must be made ready to receive a truth which, presented too suddenly, would have shattered them.

So Our Lord does not tell them at once. It is hardly an exaggeration to say that He brings them to the point where they tell Him—to Peter's "Thou art the Christ, the Son of the Living God" (Mt 16:16), to Thomas' "My Lord and my God" (Jn 20:28). Yet, from time to time, He did make statements which could only be a claim to be God.

Quite early came, "No one knows the Son but the Father, and no one knows the Father but the Son" (Mt 11:27, Lk 10:22). This is a statement of equality (and if you glance back at the chapter on the Blessed Trinity, you will see that it is precisely the Father's *knowledge* which generates the Son). Here and there as the story proceeds come other statements—note especially, "Before Abraham was made, I am" (Jn 8:58), and "The Father and I are one" (Jn 10:30).

The apostles heard these things: heard Him forgiving sins and supplementing the law God had given to Moses, always as one having in Himself total authority: saw the miracles which were the divine guarantee of His message. Yet they hesitated.

Knowing the answer, we may tend to marvel at their slowness. But, as so often happens, what kept them from the answer was that they phrased the question wrongly. They came to ask, "Was He man or was He God?" So much evidence for each possibility, and how were they to know that He was both? Who would have known *that* as a possibility, if it had not happened? What indeed does it *mean*, that one person should be man and God? The theology of the Incarnation must be our next consideration, what it means that the Word became Flesh. Never think of this as *mere* theology, a proper occupation for learned men, but too remote for us. Until we have entered deeply into it, we shall not understand anything Our Lord said or did, we shall not have the beginning of understanding of our own redemption.

Christ: God and Man

Understanding what Christ *is*—insofar as a beginning of understanding may be made here below—is essential to understanding what He *does*. We can, of course, decide not to bother with understanding, to build our whole spiritual life upon love and obedience. This attitude may be at best profound intellectual humility, at worst total intellectual unconcern. Either way it is impoverishment, a refusal of nourishment which the soul should have. To be willing to die for the truth that Christ is God is a glorious thing, but there is no glory in holding the phrase simply as a phrase, the riches in it never made our own.

Christ was a carpenter, the sort of man whom any of the neighbors could have called upon to make a plough or a doorframe. There was one such in every village of Palestine. What was special about this one is that at the same time He was infinite God, who had made all things of nothing (including the customer whose order He was executing, including indeed His own body and soul), who enlightened every man that came into this world. To say as much as this is to speak a mystery. We must begin to know what we are saying.

The key to our making the reality our own lies in the distinction between person and nature. If possible, read pages 31–38, where these terms are examined for the light they shed upon the doctrine of the Trinity. We may repeat some points of the distinction here. The nature anything has decides what it is—to take the example closest to us, we who possess a human nature, a union of spiritual soul and matter, are men. But nature, though it answers the question *what*, does not answer the question *who*. In every rational nature there is a mysterious something which says I—*that* is the person (and this is true not only for man, but for every angel, and as we have seen, for God Himself). That which says I is the person, is the answer to the question *who* any rational being is.

There is a further distinction. Nature decides what a being can do; but the person does it. My soul and body make all sorts of actions possible to me, but I do them. Whatever is done, suffered, experienced in a rational nature is done, experienced, suffered by the person whose nature it is.

Left to ourselves, we might simply assume that each person has one nature, each nature (if it happens to be rational) has one person. We have already seen how wrong we should be if we made that assumption; it is simply one more way of treating man as the measure of all. In God there is one nature, totally possessed by three distinct persons. This plurality of persons over nature is reversed in Christ Our Lord, for in Him the person is one, the natures are two.

That one Person who in Christ said I, is the Second Person of the Blessed Trinity, God the Son, God the Word. Christ is not the First Person or the Third or all three (in their profound way theologians have discussed all these as theoretical possibilities for an Incarnation different from Christ's). We have already seen why, when the first order of creation was wrecked, it fell to God the Son to make the new order. To make it, He became man: He who from eternity possessed the divine nature did, at a point of time, take to Himself and make His own a human nature, a body conceived of a woman, a soul specially created by God as our souls were.

Because Christ Our Lord, uniquely, had two natures, He could give two answers to the question "What are You?"—for nature decides what a person is. And He had two distinct principles, sources we may say, of action. By the one nature He could do all that goes with being God—He could read the heart of man for instance, He could raise Lazarus to life; by the other He could do all that goes with being man—He could be born of a mother, could hunger and thirst, could suffer, could die.

But whether He was doing the things of God or the things of man, it was always the Person who did them. Actions are always done by the person, and in Him there was but one Person. Everything He did—down to the smallest, in itself most commonplace, human act—was done by God.

Every single action of Christ was the action of the Second Person of the Blessed Trinity, and this includes every action done by Him in His human nature. For natures are sources of action, but not doers. It is always the person who does them, and in His human nature there was but one single person, and that person God. There was no human person, for that would have made Him two people, each with His own distinct nature. His human nature was complete. But it was united to a Divine Person, not a human person. He who said I in it was God, not man.

We may make this clearer by glancing at two great Christian truths—Mary was the mother of God; God died upon the Cross.

I remember the first time a street-corner heckler said to me, "If Mary was the mother of God, she must have existed *before* God." I was a newcomer to the outdoor

work of the Catholic Evidence Guild, and I simply gaped
at him. In a superior voice he went on, "You realize of
course, or don't you, that mothers come before sons?" The
immediate answer, though I did not handle the question
very brilliantly at the time, is that mothers must exist before their sons are *born*; and Our Blessed Lady did exist
before the Second Person of the Trinity was born into
human nature; that this one Son already existed in His
divine nature does not alter the truth that it was in her
womb that He was conceived as man, from her womb
born into our world. His eternal existence as Son of His
heavenly Father does not by one jot diminish what she
gave Him. There is nothing received by any human being
from his mother which He did not receive from her.

There are spiritual souls outside the Church which find
it unbearable that a woman should be mother of God: for
many such the way of escape is to speak of her as mother
of the human nature of Christ. But natures do not have
mothers. He who was born of her as man was God the
Son. She was as totally His mother as yours is yours or
mine mine.

The other truth we shall consider in this connection is
that God died upon the Cross. Here again I am reminded of
another street-corner question of about the same vintage:
"You say that God died upon the Cross; what happened
to the universe while God was dead?" The suggestion is
made that it was not God who died on Calvary, but the
humanity of Christ. But in death, it is always someone
who dies, a person; and upon Calvary's Cross, only one
Person hung, God the Son in the manhood that was His.

Thus it was God the Son who died—not, of course, in
His divine nature, which cannot know death and which
holds the universe in existence, but in the human nature
which was so utterly His. Death, remember, does not for

any one of us mean annihilation. It means the separation of soul and body, a separation which at the last judgment will be ended. Upon Calvary, the body that was God the Son's was separated from the soul that was likewise His. And on the third day thereafter they were united again. In His human nature God the Son rose from the death which in His human nature had been His.

In our reading of the Gospels, it is vital that we should never forget that every word uttered and action performed by Christ is uttered and performed by God the Son. With the words, perhaps even more than with actions, we shall find sayings we are often tempted to call hard. The one Person said I, in the divine nature and in the human nature, in an infinite nature and a finite nature. He could say, "I and the Father are one"; He could say, "The Father is greater than I"—it is the same Person, uttering the truth of distinct natures, but asserting each nature as truly His own.

We shall look further at this. Meanwhile note that one value of reading the Gospels as I have urged is the new light the reading will cast for us upon God Himself. We tend to think of the truth "Christ is God" as a piece of information about Christ, and so it is. But we shall suffer loss if we fail to see it also as information about God. Apart from it, we should know God so far as our minds are capable of seizing Him, in His own divine nature. We should know Him, for instance, as Creator of all things from nothing; although this is true, it is just a little remote, since we have no experience of creating anything from nothing. But reading the Gospels we see God in our nature, coping with our world, meeting situations known to us. Outside Christianity there is nothing to compare with the intimacy of this knowledge. It is ours for the having. It is a wonderful thing to see God being God, so to speak; but there is a special excitement in seeing God being man.

The Manhood

The Second Person of the Trinity became man. Grasp the precision of this. He did not take human nature as a mask which, when the play was over, He would triumphantly strip off. He is man in heaven and everlastingly. Nor did He simply take the appearance of a man, like the angel who guided Tobias. He did not take humanity like a garment that He could wear or an instrument that He could use. It was not simply that there were certain things He had to do which required that He must have a human body and a human soul at His disposal, and that once these things were done the whole point of having them would cease.

He became man. He is as entitled to the name as we are. As we read the Gospels, there is one single element which might make us wonder if He was wholly man—He does not sin. He Himself challenges: "Who shall convict me of sin?"; and the Epistle to the Hebrews can say (4:15), He was "tempted in all things like as we are, without sin", or, in Monsignor Knox's translation, "He had been through every trial, fashioned as we are, only sinless." But sin is not a way of being man; it is a way of misusing manhood. We misuse ours often enough, He never misused His. He was more completely man than we.

This completeness has been a profound trouble to great numbers of Christians. To them it was a beginning of trouble that God should have become man at all, but somehow they accepted it—always with the feeling that He did not really do it in its totality. Somehow they felt that the dignity of God would be safeguarded by some want of completeness in the humanity He assumed. Thus very early the Docetists taught that His body was only an appearance, whereas Saint Peter had said (1 Pet 2:24),

"Who His own self bore our sins in His body upon the Tree". But the Docetists were only a kind of crude beginning. What really started heresy after heresy was the desire to escape, not from Our Lord's body, but from His soul.

There were those who said that He had no human soul, His divinity performing the functions of a soul in the body wherein He redeemed us. The Church remembered the terrible phrase He uttered in the Garden of Gethsemane: "My soul is sorrowful even unto death." Many more people, admitting the soul, denied it intellect or will. Both these faculties are worth a closer look, if we are to grasp at once the completeness and the mysteriousness of Our Lord's humanity.

As God, Christ Our Lord was omniscient, He knew all things, His knowledge was infinite. What *could* such a person do with a finite intellect, which could only learn some tiny fraction of the things He already knew? In fact He did, and did with joy, all that could be done with it, for He was truly man. His body was real, and His senses were real; through them the external world made its way to His brain very much as it does to ours; and His human intellect proceeded to work upon their evidence as human intellects are meant to. The person who in one nature knew all things did, as Saint Luke tells us, in the other nature grow in wisdom. (Technically this is called experimental knowledge; in addition, the Church tells us, He had by God's gift two other ways of knowing: infused knowledge and the Beatific Vision. We have no space here to discuss these in detail; but observe that both are kinds of knowledge that the human soul can receive.)

Toward the end of the fifth century the Monothelites began to teach that while Our Lord had a human soul and a human intellect, He had no human will. (This was the heresy which caused a council of the Church to condemn Pope Honorius—after his death—for not condemning it with due vigor.) In a sense it is simply another form of the objection against Our Lord's finite intellect. He Himself answered it in Gethsemane when He prayed to His Father, "Not my will but thine be done." There was never the faintest disharmony between the finite will and the infinite, but one was not the other.

The real horror of this heresy, little as its adherents saw it, is that it would mean that the human heart of Christ lacked the power to love. For love is the act of the will; and whatever mystery there may be in imagining a person with an infinite intellect and a finite, an infinite will and a finite, it is simply mystery: it does not horrify us like the bleakness of a human soul that could not love.

We have begun to think of the love of Our Lord's human soul. It was, as human love must be to be wholly itself, love of God and love of man. The Gospels are filled with both.

What needs to be said about His love of man can be said quickly—it is the one thing that every Christian knows about Him, in fact that everyone knows about Him. But we have seen earlier a common misunderstanding. He is *not* a merely amiable person who goes round telling people He loves them. In fact He hardly ever tells anyone that. There is not a trace of sentimentality in Him, no sugar at all. His speech is abrupt, realistic, not often melting. It was not from His speech that men learned His love for them: it was above all from His actions. But learn it they did; and it was one of His disciples who uttered what is perhaps the most wonderful phrase of all religion, "God is love." Saint John was combining the two truths he had come to know, that Christ is God and Christ is love.

What will startle the reader coming new to the Gospels is the intensity of Our Lord's devotion to His Father in heaven. The first words recorded of Him are, "Did you not know that I must be about my Father's business?"; His last words on the Cross were, "Father, into thy hands I commend my spirit." In between, His love for the Father is continually finding expression. Time and again we are told that He went apart from the apostles to pray to His heavenly Father.

Here we come to the third form of a difficulty which we have already considered twice. How can a person pray, when He is Himself God? Every act of Our Lord, whether in the divine nature or the human, was the act of the Person that He was. When Christ prayed, it was the Second Person of the Trinity who prayed. And prayer is, of its very essence, the utterance of the finite creature to the infinite God. Once again we face mystery, yet some small gleam of light we can get. It is the function, the duty, of a person to utter his nature; having taken and made His own a human nature, God the Son must utter it, and this includes uttering its adoration and thanksgiving and petition. But realize that though it was truly human prayer, it could not be simply as the prayer of men who are no more than men. Our Lord could teach His apostles to pray; but He never prayed with them.

Because He had a real soul and a real body, Our Lord had real emotions too. Love, for instance, can be perfectly real simply as the total turning of the will to the good of others, without having any emotional accompaniment. Angels, we are told, love like that. But it is an odd man who has never known the emotion of love, a man, in that at least, not like Our Lord. He loved, and must have shown His love for, one of His disciples—Saint John is especially "the disciple whom Jesus loved"; and one gets an overwhelming sense of His love for the family at Bethany, Lazarus and Martha and Mary.

He wept, too; not only over Lazarus of Bethany but over Jerusalem. And He could storm in anger. The long attack quoted by Saint Matthew upon the Pharisees is the very high point of invective, justified invective, stimulating perhaps to us who are not Pharisees, but terrifying to every man who has ever examined his own conscience.

The temptation is to continue with the Man we meet in the Gospels. Let us consider one final question which in a way is a summarization of what we have been discussing. What does a Person who is God *do* with a human soul?

Clearly He does with it all that can be done with it, using every power it has to the uttermost of its possibility. And that is something that no merely human person has ever done. Most of us use our minds when we have to, under compulsion so to speak, and not very brilliantly. The geniuses of our race are a constant reminder of our own mediocrity. But not the greatest genius does all with his soul that can, by the uttermost use of its own possibilities, be done. In fact, men do show a certain development in their realization of the human soul's possibilities; there have been very considerable advances in the last hundred years in the understanding of the mind's powers. Men have glimpsed the possibility of a profounder control, for instance, of soul over body. Our Lord had to wait for none of this. For He had made that soul of His, and it had no hidden surprises for Him. He knew what it could do.

He could do all that could be done with His human soul—but not more! We have seen that man's destiny is to do something which by nature he cannot do—see the face of God. He cannot do it, not because his own use of his nature is defective, but because unaided human nature cannot do it. That superb, that incomparable soul of Christ was given sanctifying grace. It was, as every spiritual soul should be, indwelt by the Holy Spirit.

XII

REDEMPTION

Suffering and Death

Once we have come to some understanding of who and
what the Redeemer is, we are in a better condition to see
into the meaning of redemption.

For the state from which mankind needed to be
redeemed it would be well to reread the chapter on the
Fall of Man. Here we may summarize briefly the principal
element in it. Owing to the sin of the first man, the race
had lost its union with God; a breach lay between. Where
God and man had been at one, they were now at two: till
at-one-ment, atonement, was made, heaven was closed to
the race's members.

God could, of course, have simply written off the race
as a failure. He could, as simply, have forgiven the sin. He
did neither. He chose that in human nature the sin committed in human nature should be expiated.

For the act by which Christ redeemed us was a wholly
human act. The life He offered as sacrifice was His human
life; an offering of the divine life would have been meaningless. The suffering was in His soul and body; the death
was the separation of His soul and body.

In Him, humanity gave its all, holding back nothing.
Here was a total obedience as against the disobedience of
man's sin, a total acceptance and self-surrender as against

the thrust and self-assertion of man's sin. And all this was wholly in human nature.

But He who performed the act was God: actions, we have seen, are always in the nature, but the person does them: and the Person whose human nature this was, in whose human nature all this was done, was, is, God the Son. Because He was truly man, His sacrifice was truly human, so that it could be set against the sin of the race. But because He was God, His act had an infinite value, by which it compensated, outweighed, not only all the sin men ever had committed but all they ever could. That, in essence, is why it is redemptive.

Every act of Christ was infinite in value because He who performed it was God. Why then did He offer His death, and not some lesser act—the tears, for example, that He shed over Jerusalem? It is always perilous to think one knows why God does one thing and not another. His ways are unsearchable, our mind is not His.

But at least we can say that had He chosen some offering less than His life, there would have been a permanent feeling in the mind of man—not dissatisfaction exactly, but not total satisfaction either. We should have been left with the sense that in our redemption Christ's human nature had played only a token part, leaving the infinity of the Divine Person to do the whole work. Whereas He chose that His human nature should give its all, leaving the Person to provide only the infinite value which human nature never could provide.

Observe the words "He chose". No man could inflict death upon Him against His will. He says again and again that He would "lay down" His life for His sheep. "I am laying down my life to take it up again afterwards. Nobody can rob me of it; I lay it down of my own accord" (Jn 10:17–18). He did not choose that men should slay Him, of course. But since men willed to slay Him because He had fearlessly spoken the word of God against them, He chose to let them do the worst that was in them. Through love, He Himself would be the victim offered in sacrifice: they would slay Him, He would offer His death for the sins of all men, including theirs.

It is essential at this point to reread what Matthew (Chapter 26), Mark (Chapter 14) and Luke (Chapter 22) have to tell us of the Agony in the Garden.

He would take upon Himself the sins of men that the offering He made of Himself might be real expiation. In Gethsemane we get some glimpse of what the taking meant to Him. For nothing He does is fiction or pretense. He could not make His own the guilt of other men's sins, for guilt can be only in the sinner. But He took the burden of them, the weight: above all the weight of the sorrow that we, all men, should have felt for our sins and have not felt. It all but killed Him.

But His Father, answering His agonized prayer, sent an angel "to comfort Him". For that hour He lived. Death waited for Calvary.

Passion, Resurrection and Ascension

In the Ordinary of the Mass a grouping of words occurs twice which, unless we realize that in the Liturgy no word is wasted, we might simply take in our stride, not noticing the remarkable thing it is saying. (I for one thus took it in my stride for thirty years or thereabouts.)

Between the Washing of the Hands and the Orate Fratres the priest asks the Holy Trinity to receive "this oblation which we offer to Thee in memory of the Passion, Resurrection and Ascension of Our Lord Jesus Christ".

After the Consecration the priest says that we offer the sacrifice in memory, not of Christ's Passion only, but also of His Resurrection from the grave and, as well, of His glorious Ascension into heaven.

The point of each is the same, but emphasized more strongly in the second: the sacrifice commemorates not only the suffering and death on Calvary, but the Resurrection and Ascension as well. The Resurrection is not simply a sign that one man has conquered death; the Ascension is not simply a way of letting the apostles know that their Christ had really left this world. Both have their function, along with Calvary, in our redemption. Both belong to the completeness of the sacrifice by which the breach between the race and God was healed, grace was set flowing in a vast new abundance, heaven was opened to the members of the race.

Let us pause a moment upon this Sacrifice: for us it is of all actions the highest, since by it our race was redeemed. From the beginning men, though they did not know what ultimately would be wrought by it, still saw sacrifice as the highest act of religion. It was a public act, a ritual act, performed by one for the people; by it something was withdrawn from man's personal use, made sacred, offered to God in profession that all man had was God's.

Of course that man should offer is not the whole story; unless God approves and accepts, all is vain. There were occasions in the Old Testament where God showed His approval publicly—as by sending fire from heaven upon the offering.

But only in the supreme sacrifice of our redemption does God show His approval and acceptance publicly, totally. In the Resurrection God gives the visible sign that the Priest who offered His own body and blood in sacrifice was wholly pleasing to Him. In the Ascension God shows visibly that He is actually taking to Himself that which has been offered to Him.

Christ ascends to His Father, to be with Him forever, with the marks of His sacrifice still, but now glorious, in His body—the everlasting reminder that man's sin has been expiated, that the breach has been closed between God and man, that they are again as they were in the beginning of man, at one. So the Epistle to the Hebrews (7:25) shows Christ in heaven, "ever living to make intercession for us".

At the Last Supper, Our Lord had told the apostles that He must go; and, answering their anguish, he gives as the all-sufficient reason that if He does not go, the Holy Spirit will not come. For Christ, everything is in that. The order broken by Adam's sin has been re-established, or rather, a better order has been established: that was for the Second Person. Now is the time for such a rich flowing of gifts as the souls of men have never known. And gifts are the fruit of love, and so are appropriated to the Third Person, who within the Blessed Trinity is the uttered love of the First Person and the Second.

At the Last Supper Christ had promised His followers that when He went to the Father, He would send the Holy Spirit. At the Ascension, on the point of going to the Father He tells them to return to Jerusalem, and await the Holy Spirit's coming. Ten days later He descended upon them—on Pentecost (the word means "Fiftieth", summing the forty days from Resurrection to Ascension, and the ten days from that).

Before proceeding to the great question of how we are to be made partakers of Christ's redemptive act, we may cast a brief glance at the Vanquished in the great conflict fought upon Calvary, the one who had been victorious in that first conflict in the dawn of our history—Satan.

It has already been noted that as the Passion draws near, Our Lord is continually conscious of *the* Enemy, mentioning Satan again and again. Satan was conscious of Christ too, but he did not know Christ as Christ knew him. It is ironical that he rushed upon his defeat—for, we are told by Saint Luke and Saint John, it was he who moved Judas to betray the Lord to His slayers.

Truth, Life, Union

At the Last Supper Our Lord uttered the words which are at once the formula of our redemption, and the charter of His Church. "I am the way and the truth and the life. No man cometh unto the Father but by me."

It is possible to have known and loved the phrase all one's life, yet not have given much actual thought to what it contains; there is so much splendor in the saying that one may fail to grasp what is being said. To anyone whose experience this has so far been, it will be valuable to pause now and make his own examination of those superb words, before going on to read mine.

A first thought may be of wonder why, if Our Lord is the Way, there is need for more: why are Truth and Life added? If He is the Way, when you have found Him you have found all. But the two additional words are there to challenge us. With them we are face to face with a reality at once frightening and stimulating. It is the reality Saint Paul expressed: "Work out your salvation with fear and trembling" (Phil 2:12).

Salvation is not handed to us on a platter: in no sense is it a labor-saving device. What Christ does for men is what men cannot do for themselves, not what they can: what they can, they should. To have found the Way is not the end, it is the beginning. The Way is not the Goal. Only the Goal is, for us, permanence: the Way may be lost.

We might lose the Way, as we might lose any way, either by wandering from it through error, or by lacking the strength for the effort—"the fear and trembling"—that following it to the end demands. As against the danger of losing the Way we need Truth. As against the danger of falling by the wayside we need Life—Our Lord came that we might have Life "and more abundantly" (Jn 10:10)—the life of sanctifying grace.

And what in any event does Our Lord mean by calling Himself the Way? He tells us the answer Himself: "no man cometh unto the Father but by me." It is in union with Him, and only so, that men come to that everlasting union with God which is their destiny.

Salvation then involves truth, life, union with the God-man. How these are to be ours He tells in the words He utters on a mountain in Galilee between His rising from the dead and His rising into heaven to present before the throne of God the sacrifice of our salvation. To the apostles—the eleven still with Him—He says: "Go and teach all nations; baptizing them in the name of the Father and of the Son and of the Holy Spirit; teaching them to observe all things whatsoever I have commanded. And behold, I am with you all days even to the end of the world" (Mt 28:19–20).

Observe how closely this follows the great formula of the Last Supper—truth, life, union.

Truth first. They are to *teach*, and teach all things. He had told them earlier (Mt 13:11) that whereas He had taught the rest in parables, to them He spoke plainly. He had promised them at the Last Supper (Jn 16:13) that when the Holy Spirit came He should lead them into all truth: How? By bringing to their mind all that Our Lord had told them. And now they were to teach this great mass of truth to all nations.

Next, life. They were to baptize: baptism means being born again of water and the Holy Spirit (Jn 3:5). To be born means to enter into the life of this world. To be born again means to enter into a higher life. And these were the men to whom He had given other powers for the dispensing of life. They were to forgive sins (Jn 20:23): that is, to give back the life of grace to those who had lost it by sin. And they were to change bread and wine into His Body and Blood—the very food of our life: for He had said to the multitudes, "Unless you shall eat the flesh of the Son of man and drink His blood you shall not have life in you" (Jn 6:54).

What of union? Look again. "Behold *I am with you* all days even to the end of the world."

Through the apostles—and, since it was to be until the world should end, through their successors—we were to find the truth, the life, the union by which we shall be saved.

XIII

THE VISIBLE CHURCH

The Structure of the Church

Man's salvation, we have seen, was bound up with the apostles. Through them Christ's teaching and Christ's life would be given to men till the end of time. He would be with the apostles, which means two things principally—first, in union with them we are in union with Him; second, He guarantees the teaching they give and the life they dispense to us.

This is the Church He had promised to found upon Peter. This is the Church upon which the Holy Spirit descended in the form of tongues of fire ten days later. There were eleven apostles; and one of them, Peter, as we shall see in more detail later, was to be the shepherd who should represent here on earth the Good Shepherd who had ascended to His Father. There were a hundred and twenty disciples: "disciple" means "learner": "apostle" means one who is "sent"—sent to bear the gifts of truth and life and union.

That was the Church which was "born of the Holy Spirit and of fire" on the first Pentecost day. There would be developments in the structure—there would, for instance, be new officials subordinate to the apostles, as the growth in the numbers of disciples called for increasing complexity in administration. But the main lines of the structure are established for all time—the body of disciples, the dispensers of truth and life, the one man who represented Christ as Shepherd of the Flock.

At all these levels the human beings will change, as men die and are replaced by others. But the same Christ will be in operation. The Church, united with Him, is doing in His power the things He had done for men in His body, as He wants them done now. The same Holy Spirit who indwelt Him indwells His Church.

We see Our Lord's mind upon all this most clearly if we look at what He made of Peter. The first strong hint is in the changing of his name from Simon to Peter, which means rock; with the meaning of the change made clear in Matthew (16:17–20)—"Thou art Peter and upon this rock I will build my Church...." If you do not know the words by memory, reread the passage now.

Read too what Our Lord said to Peter at the Last Supper (Lk 22:28–32). We may concentrate here upon the words in which Christ makes Peter to be the shepherd of the flock (Jn 21:15–18). In three phrases Peter is told that *he* must feed the lambs and the sheep. This involves a command to the whole flock to be fed by him. But with what food?

Three times Our Lord speaks of food. To the Devil tempting Him He quotes Deuteronomy: "Man does not live by bread alone but by every word that proceeds from the mouth of God": so what God speaks is food.

To His disciples urging Him to eat (Jn 4:34), He says, "My meat is to do the will of Him that sent me": so the divine law is food.

And to the multitude whom He had fed with five loaves and two fishes He had said (Jn 6:55), "The man who eats my flesh and drinks my blood enjoys eternal life, and I will raise him up at the Last Day": so His Body and Blood are food.

With truth and law and sacrament Peter must see to it that we are fed—Peter and the men who one by one shall succeed him as shepherds till the end of time.

Yet not by their own power. After each of the commissions He gave to Peter, Our Lord added a rebuke. In Matthew 16, He says *to Peter*, "Get thee behind me, Satan", for Peter was urging Him not to go to Jerusalem and suffer. In Luke 22, there is almost worse: "before the cock crows, thou shalt deny me thrice." And there is a strange phrase near the end of John 21: "What is it to thee?"

Peter became a saint; many of his successors have been canonized too; many startle us by their small show of sanctity. So with bishops and priests. We rejoice in the evidently holy, we may be sad at others. But the power in which, by which, we live is never theirs. It is always Christ's. It is Christ we join when we join the Church, not the men who at any given moment direct it here upon earth. The gifts come to us through them: but always from Him.

The Church Is Catholic and Apostolic

Christ, then, had chosen that His work for the redemption of men should be carried on while the world should last—by Himself, of course, but through a society of men. He had promised Peter (Mt 16–18) that He should build the Church upon him, and Peter must have been at once delighted and puzzled, wondering what this Church might be.

With the words uttered so near to Our Lord's Ascension into heaven (Mt 28:19–20), the nature, purpose and structure of the Church were made clear. Peter and the other apostles were to be its key men; till the end of time it would be apostolic. And till the end of time it would be catholic.

The glory of this last word is inexhaustible. Here we must be content to look at its bare meaning. Catholic, we say, is from a Greek word meaning universal. What does universal mean? The word contains two elements—all and one, all in one.

In His first commission to Peter, Our Lord had made clear what He meant by "one"—His Church was to be built upon the Rock, Peter was to have the keys and a power of binding and loosing which God Himself would ratify. In His final commission to the apostles, He made clear what He meant by "all"—a threefold all: all nations, all doctrines, all ages.

When we say the Nicene Creed we call the Church "one, holy, Catholic and apostolic". Rightly we speak of these as her four marks. Pause upon the marks. They mean outward showings, visible to anyone who troubles to look; they do not require the eye of faith, any rational observer can see that they are there. He may not see the importance the Catholic sees in them, but once he knows what we mean by the marks, the qualities outwardly shown, he will admit that the Church does actually show them.

For the Catholic they are immeasurably more than that—they are the outward showings of inner realities. The showing can vary from age to age, according as men respond well or ill to the gifts of Christ. But the inner reality abides changeless; Christ made His Church thus, it can never be otherwise.

The Church has the mark of catholicity, for example: as the ages have passed between her foundation and now, she has in fact taught all doctrines to nations beyond number.

But in her inmost reality, she is no more catholic now than when she was founded.

When Our Lord established the Church, it consisted of one hundred and twenty Jews; it had no age at all, its teaching had not begun. And in that instant it was the *Catholic* Church. For it had been made by the universal Teacher and Lifegiver for all men. *That* is the inner reality, of which the mark began to show as early as Pentecost Day.

The mark has been more spectacularly in evidence at some times than at others; nations have joined the Church, nations have left it. But it is always the Church through which Our Lord offers men the fullness of truth and life and union.

The inner reality is of the essence; but the outward showings are of immense importance as establishing the Church's special and unique relation to God.

As a mark, apostolicity is seen in a variety of ways, notably three. First, the Church goes back in an unbroken line to the one that came to life in our world on the first Pentecost; by the laying-on of hands every bishop, every priest is linked with the apostles. Second, the Church, like the apostles, teaches and has always taught whatever Christ taught; at no point has it ever been conceived, for example, that with the progress of learning we know better than He. There has been development, but always a genuine development of what He gave. Third, the Church teaches *as* the apostles taught, that is with complete authority; at every age she has said what the apostles said at the Council of Jerusalem (Acts 15:28) "It hath seemed good to the Holy Spirit and to us."

Two points may be worth noting about the mark of catholicity. Every sort of nation has joined the Church, each feeling wholly at home. And every sort of man in every nation has joined it, lived in it and loved it. There is no such thing as a Catholic type. There are vast differences between centuries and civilizations and nations and individuals; the Church is able to get down below the differences to that in humanity which all men have. Naturally, for she is made by the God who made men.

The Church Is One

The mark of unity comes naturally to the mind after a discussion of catholicity, which would indeed be pointless without it. To be catholic and not one would have no meaning at all.

The importance of unity in Our Lord's sight comes out unmistakably in a phrase He uses at the Last Supper (Jn 17:22). He had prayed for the apostles, then for all those who through their teaching might come to accept Himself—

"that they may be one
as Thou Father in Me and I in Thee,
that they may be one in us
that the world may know that Thou hast sent me."

Unity meant so much *to Him* that upon it He was prepared to stake the proof to the world of His own divinity. And it meant so much *in itself* that He could compare it to the unity within the Godhead of the First Person and the Second.

Look at the words again. The unity was to be of men in the Trinity—"that they may be one in us": that is the inner reality. But it must be outwardly visible, that the world might see it as evidence of the inner reality of Christ: that is the mark.

Catholics, we say, are united in faith, worship and government.

In faith—the doctrines to be believed and the spiritual and moral laws to be obeyed they accept from the Church as Christ teaching and commanding.

In worship, similarly, they accept the Mass and the sacraments as through the Church but from Christ.

The third of this trio, government, may be seen most simply in what Our Lord said, first to Peter alone (Mt 16:19) then to all the apostles together (Mt 18:18): "Whatsoever you shall bind on earth shall be bound also in heaven." Within the framework of the moral, spiritual, ritual laws actually given by Christ, the Church may make regulations to aid her members to live more fully in accord with them. Examples are her laws upon fasting before Communion, upon mixed marriage, upon celibacy of the clergy.

Only a habit of skipping the unfamiliar can account for any lover of the Gospels finding the Church's unity unattractive. Yet to many it is plainly repulsive. They see it as regimentation, tyranny in the rulers, servility in the ruled. The worst political evil of the day has provided them with a name for it—totalitarianism.

Totalitarianism is precisely what it is not. For in the totalitarian state, everything is under the control of the state, there is no private sphere; whereas in the Church the distinction is clean-drawn between the religious sphere and the civil; and in the civil sphere the Church claims no authority over her members.

There have been occasions of real overlap, civil questions having direct religious effects; and others of genuine difference of opinion as to which authority is entitled to act. But over the long run of history, even its opponents do not find the Church much given to laying down the law in the civil sphere—in America or England, to take countries familiar to ourselves, the Pope has never told Catholics how to vote in an election.

There is a feeling that one who makes all his own decisions in religion is freer and more natural. But if a man joins, or remains in, the Church because he believes Christ founded it to give us truth and life and union with Him, then it is mere sanity to accept the doctrines and the moral laws it tells us Christ has given it, and the means of life and union. It is not as if we could discover these things for ourselves. We know them on God's revelation or not at all. We must find the teacher authorized by God to teach and accept his authority. The alternative is to go without. And freedom is not served by ignorance.

The Church Is Holy

With the mark of holiness as with the others, we must distinguish between the outward showing—visible to anyone who cares to look and liable to grow greater or less—and the inner characteristic, visible to the eye of faith and belonging to the Church's very essence, present from the first moment of her existence and never varying.

In this profounder sense the holiness of the Church is simply the holiness of Christ. It is His Church, made by Him as the bearer of holiness to men. Every member, in contact with Him, has available to him a fount of holiness; there is no limit save our own will to receive what He has to give.

There is no growth and, of course, no diminishing. If every one of her members were in a state of grace at a given moment, the Church's holiness would be no greater; if we were all in mortal sin together, it would be no less. In other words the holiness of the Church is not the sum

total of the holiness of all her members, any more than
the wetness of rain is measured by the wetness of all those
who have ventured out in it. If the whole population goes
out and gets drenched, the rain is no wetter; if everyone
stays indoors, the rain is no less wet. Rain is wet because it
is rain, whether or not men expose themselves to it. The
Church is holy because it is Christ living on in the world.
It is the cause of the holiness of its members, but is not
measured by their response.

But with the *mark*, we find ourselves looking at the
effects upon the members, so far as these are outwardly
visible. The Church can be seen to be holy because she
teaches a holy doctrine, she offers to all the means of holiness, and the saints are there to show how immeasurably
effective these means can be. All three are vast topics. We
can at least glance at them.

That she teaches a holy doctrine we know, in the fullness of its reality, by faith. But even one who has no faith,
and either differs from the Church as to what constitutes
holiness or even dismisses holiness as of no account in a
busy world, can see one plain fact. In her teaching she
always cleaves to her own standard of holiness—that the
will of God is absolute. She never allows deviation from
it for any reason whatsoever; worldly advantage, human
weakness, she knows about these things; but she never
allows them to affect her utterance of God's law.

She has had popes who made no fetish of personal holiness, but not one of them ever tried to reword the law of
God to allow for the indulgence of his own temptations.
And no other human quality has ever taken precedence of
holiness. Her heroes are the saints: she inserts into her liturgy masses for saints, but not for individual popes, however great, unless they too happened to be saints. And if
anyone be tempted to smile cynically at that last word,

remember that only [as of 1957] two popes of the last four hundred years have been canonized.

Of the means of holiness as of the teaching, the same distinction must be drawn between what her members know by faith and their own experience, and what is plainly visible to anyone who cares to look.

Of this latter sort are, to pluck a few almost at random, the ways in which she aids her members to live according to the holiness she has taught them. Even one who does not believe in sacramental confession must at least admit that the Church which requires it takes the battle with sin seriously. The daily examination of conscience she urges upon us witnesses in the same direction, as do the annual or more frequent retreats that she provides.

There is no take-it-or-leave-it about the Church's condemnation of sin and urging to holiness. Consider another thing: the spiritual writings of her greatest children are read not only by her own members, but by men of all faiths. Saint Augustine's *Confessions*, *The Imitation of Christ*, Saint Francis de Sales' *Introduction to the Devout Life* are read by Christians outside the Church as they read no books by writers of their own faith.

One more of the means, or aids, to holiness offered by the Church to her members is especially worth mention, because it is of the first practical importance and is not always realized in this particular connection. It is the example of the saints.

The abiding temptation of every Christian is to feel that the standard set by Christ is high and holy, but quite simply beyond our powers: it is splendid but impossible. The feeling is foolish, of course. The God who made men would not know so little of the beings He made as to ask the impossible of them. But knowing it foolish does not diminish its force. We feel that however it may be for others, our peculiar circumstances and difficulties make the living of Christ's life impossible for us.

Here is a special value of the saints. Men and women of our own sort, in our circumstances, beset by our difficulties, have attained high and heroic sanctity. As this comes home to us, holiness will still seem difficult, but it will no longer seem impossible. And between the difficult and the impossible there is all the difference in the world.

It may seem at once ungracious and merely silly to tell other Christian religions their business. I can simply utter my own wonder at how they get on without something equivalent to the canonization of saints. It would, I should think, be a help to a Methodist or Presbyterian, tempted as he feels beyond his strength, to read of a Methodist store-keeper of the eighteenth century, a Presbyterian farmer's daughter of the nineteenth, who overcame the same difficulties as his or hers and became a great saint.

For the men and women canonized by the Church are of every sort, rich and poor, learned and ignorant, powerfully tempted or hardly at all, people of evil life who have repented, people who from infancy have not deviated from the love of God and neighbor. It is no exaggeration to say that the saints are as various, as catholic in that sense, as the Church itself.

Three characteristics of the mark of holiness are, as has been said, the teaching, the means, the saints. It may have been noticed that, in treating the first two, the teaching and the means, we brought in the saints; it may be wondered what is left to say of them in the third. But in all three characteristics they are used differently. In the teaching we saw them as the unchanging standard the Church sets; in the means, we saw them as witness to our weakness that holiness is possible even to us.

Now, at last, we come to them as evidence to the whole world that the teaching is true teaching and the means are effective means. For the saints are the people who have accepted wholeheartedly all that Christ, through His Church, offers them.

In other words, it is by the saints, and not by the mediocre, still less by the great sinners, that the Church is to be judged. It may seem a loading of the dice to demand that any institution be judged solely by its best members, but in this instance it is not. A medicine must be judged not by those who buy it but by those who actually take it. A Church must be judged by those who hear and obey, not by those who half-hear and disobey when obedience is difficult.

No Catholic is compelled—not by the Church, not by Christ—to be holy. His will is solicited, aided, not forced.

In Francis Thompson's words the Church is not a machine

> "To pack and label men for God
> And save them by the barrel-load".

Every man must make his own response. The saints have responded totally; the rest of us respond partially, timorously (afraid to lose some sin in which we especially delight), or not at all. The saints in their thousands upon thousands stand as proof that, in the Church, holiness is to be had for the willing. Every saint is certain evidence that, if you and I are not saints, the choice is wholly our own.

We have come to an end of our consideration of the marks of the Church. The point throughout has been to get at what the inner reality is which the marks outwardly show. What should be clear is that in every case the inner reality is some special way in which Christ Our Lord functions in the Church. There is in fact a deeper presence of Christ than we have yet stated. To that we must now come.

The Teaching of Truth

On a hillside in Galilee, between the Resurrection and the Ascension, Our Lord had told the apostles to teach all nations. They were to teach all that He had taught them, all doctrines, all laws. And He promised to be with them all days till time should end. Thus the apostles, protected by Christ Himself in their utterance of His teaching, were to have successors, likewise protected. That was Christ's plan that men should have truth here upon earth.

It seems strange that a large number of Christians think the apostles fulfilled their commission by writing the New Testament, leaving behind them no successors, or any need for successors, with the authority Our Lord had given themselves. It seems strange for one reason, that it would mean only four of the apostles had obeyed their Master—Matthew writing a gospel, John a gospel and three brief letters, Peter two letters and Jude one. Not a written word from Thomas, for instance, so ready with his tongue—I at least would be willing to give up the great book of his greatest namesake to have one about Christ from him!

It would seem strange for another reason—that the Church Christ founded would have been a teaching Church only for a half century or so, in all the centuries since merely a library. Circumstances change and someone must have authority to apply the teachings to the new circumstances, otherwise they would end up as frustrations rather than teachings. Even in the doctrines themselves there are depths which the believing mind can explore, with all the danger of error but all the rich possibilities of development. With every operation of the unstagnant mind of man upon the truth, the question must arise, "What did Christ mean?"

So it has proved. There is not a word uttered by Christ which has not met a great number of diverse interpretations, some of them intelligent, some immensely attractive, but contradicting each other. How are we to know? It is not enough to have Our Lord's words; the words themselves can be only a kind of talisman without the meaning. Without a teacher who can tell us, beyond the possibility of error, which of the various meanings is Christ's? We have no revelation but only an ever-growing pile of conundrums.

Either there is a teacher now teaching upon earth, guaranteed by Christ as the apostles were, or there is no possibility of knowing the truth which He saw to be so essential. Already, well before His death, He had given men authority to teach with His authority—it was to the disciples, not the apostles only, that He said "He that hears you, hears me." That, extended to the Church He founded for all ages, is His formula to ensure that we shall receive His truth with no admixture of error. There is no other. The name for it is infallibility.

This, in brief, is the way of it. The successors of the apostles are the bishops. What they are agreed in teaching as the Revelation of Christ upon faith and morals—that is upon truths to be believed and laws to be obeyed—is infallible: God sees to it that it contains no error. The agreement referred to need not be total, including every single bishop that has been or now is; individual bishops in some time or place may teach error. But what may be called a moral universality—a teaching given by the great mass of the bishops of the world—is certainly true.

This teaching by bishops is the normal way in which Our Lord's Revelation reaches the Catholic. But where it is uncertain what the bishops are agreed in teaching, or where either some new problem arises calling for new clarification or some new heresy arises calling for a more precise statement of the denied truth, there is what we may think of as a court of last resort. In the words of the Vatican Definition of 1870, the Pope "is endowed with that infallibility with which it has pleased God to endow His Church". If the Pope issues to the whole Church a solemn definition of revealed truth, then that too is certain. He that hears him, hears Christ.

Infallibility is concerned with teaching only. It is no guarantee of the Pope's holiness. As a matter of fact the Popes whose concern with holiness is less obvious have not been much given to infallible definitions. But, whether or no, the exclusion of error is not due to any human virtue; it is solely the act of God.

XIV

THE MYSTICAL BODY OF CHRIST

We have taken a first look at the Church Our Lord established. We have seen that in it and through it we have access to the truth and the life and the union with Himself in which our redemption consists. What truth means has been explained fairly fully, and something has been said of life, though more must be said. But what of union?

From what has been said thus far, we see it as a union of love and obedience. And as such it is wonderful beyond man's dreams. But that is only the fringe. The fullness of the union that Christ planned for us—union with Himself and through Him with God—is far closer and deeper. We must try to understand it, for it is the central reality of the Church and the central reality of ourselves. (For a fuller study of the Church, as visible body and Mystical Body, a wonderful book is Karl Adam's *Spirit of Catholicism*.)

Take as a starting point the question Our Lord, from the right hand of His Father in heaven, put to Saul on the road to Damascus. (Read Acts 9:1–8.) Saul had been persecuting the Christians in Jerusalem fiercely (for he never did anything by halves, either as Saul the Pharisee or Paul the Apostle). He was on his way to Damascus to seize Christians there too when he was stricken blind and heard a voice saying: "Saul, Saul, why are you persecuting Me?" Not My Church, you observe, but *Me*.

Our Lord is asserting an *identity* between His Church and Himself. Is it a real identity—that is, does He mean the words to be taken at their full value? Or is it merely a rhetorical device, a way of saying that the Church is His special property, so that if anyone persecutes it, it is *as though* he persecuted Him? It would have been an odd moment for rhetoric: for Saul it was the moment of truth. He knew the identity to be real. Years later he could write to the Galatians (3:28): "You are all one person in Jesus Christ."

Our Lord had actually said it—although on the Damascus road Saul knew nothing of that—at the Last Supper: or rather on the way from the Supper room to the Garden of Gethsemane (Jn 15:5): "I am the Vine, you are the branches."

The phrase is decisive. The union of Christians with Christ is no mere union of love and obedience; it is a living, organic unity. Branches are not simply a society that the vine decides to found and take a kindly interest in. The vine lives in the branches, the branches live in the vine, live with the very life of the vine.

Our union with Christ is of such a sort that He lives in us, we live in Him, live with His very life.

The truth is at once marvelous and mysterious. It is Saint Paul who goes deepest into the mystery—naturally, because it alone Our Lord had uttered in converting him. The Church is the body of Christ and we are all members of His body, parts of His body. With our present knowledge of the human body's structure we more readily think of ourselves as cells in His body. We shall return to Saint Paul later: here note one text (1 Cor 12:27): "You are Christ's body, organs of it depending upon each other."

We have come to call the Church the Mystical Body of Christ: the adjective simply means mysterious. Thus we distinguish it from the natural body, in which He was conceived in the womb of His Mother and born in Bethlehem, which hung upon the Cross, is now at the right hand of the Father, is received by us under the appearance of bread in the Eucharist. Theologians speak of the second Body as the successor of the first, because in it Our Lord continues to act among men as He did in His natural body during His short life upon earth.

To call the Church Christ's Body is no more a piece of rhetoric than was His own phrase to Saul. The Church is not simply an organization to which we resort for the gifts He wants us to have; to think of it only as a society founded by Him is not enough. In our human experience a living body comes closest to giving us the true idea of it. For it is of the essence of a living body that there is one life-center, so that every element in it lives by one same life.

That we are thus living cells in a body of which Christ is head is the most important fact about ourselves. We must try to see further into it.

To the Ephesians, Saint Paul said (1:22): "God made Christ the head to which the whole Church is joined, so that the Church is his body."

In other words Our Lord, living in His natural body in heaven, lives also in another body on earth. The second body is not a replica of the first, it is of a different order. But it is as truly entitled to be called both a body, and Christ's body. In a body, every element, every limb and organ, every cell lives with one same life, the life of him whose body it is. So it is with Christ's natural body, so it is with His Mystical Body.

The two lives are different: in the first body it is natural life, in the second supernatural life, sanctifying grace. In the Church every member has his own natural life and must labor to correct its defects; but the life of grace, by which at last we shall come to the vision of God in heaven—that is simply Christ living in us, sharing His own life with us. "I live," says Saint Paul, "now not I, but Christ lives in me."

We have cells in our own body living with our life; we must become cells in Christ's body, living with His. We must be incorporated with Christ, built into His body. How? By baptism. Born into the race of Adam, we must be reborn into Christ. "We were taken up into Christ by baptism", says Saint Paul to the Romans (6:3); to the Galatians he says (3:27), "All you who have been baptized in Christ's name have put on the person of Christ ... you are all one person in Christ."

That, then, is the Church; and that is what it is to belong to the Church. We are built into, in that sense made one with, Our Lord's humanity. But that humanity is the humanity of God the Son; so that we are united with the Second Person and thus with the Blessed Trinity. We now see new meaning in two phrases used by Our Lord at the Last Supper.

In a text already quoted, He prays that all who come to accept Him "may be one, as Thou Father in Me and I in Thee, that they also may be one in us" (Jn 17:21, but read on to the end of the chapter). Near the beginning of the great discourse He had uttered the same truth in one phrase, "I am in My Father and you in Me and I in you" (Jn 14:20).

To be a Catholic and not to grasp what it is to be a Catholic—that is a matter for pity, one misses so much. But to grasp it can be frightening too, for we have not only the supernatural life given us by Christ, we have also natural life of our own and in harmonizing nature and grace few of us can show any spectacular success. Yet with all our mediocrity there is greatness for us: there is no other dignity given to men which can approach this, and it is given to every one of us by baptism.

We are united with Christ, who is God, with a closeness which no human relationship even comes near. Mother and son are close, but they are still two. Our union with Christ is closer than that union, at its very closest, could ever be: and this for a double reason.

First we are members of Christ—we do not think of the organs of our own body, heart or liver for instance, as relations, kinsmen; they are closer to our very being and so are we to Christ's.

Second our union with Christ is in the supernatural order, and the lowest relation in the order of grace is nearer than the highest in the order of nature. It was so for Our Lady herself. Saint Augustine notes that she was more exalted by her holiness than by her relation to Our Lord: and he says again, "More blessed was Mary in receiving Christ's faith than in conceiving Christ's flesh."

Even when we have grasped the reality of the Mystical Body, most of us know that we are making scarcely an effort to live up to it. Take one single fact: every Catholic is closer to us by the union he and we have with Christ than is any member of our family by natural kinship. If we began to treat one another accordingly, it would be a new world.

To treat another Catholic with cruelty or injustice is plainly to act as if the Mystical Body did not exist; but short of actual maltreatment, to regard a fellow member of Christ's body as merely somebody else is to ignore the principal fact about ourself and him.

We have just spoken of Our Lady. She is the first member of the Mystical Body. We shall speak more of her.

XV

THE MOTHER OF GOD

The Son Who Chose His Mother

Our understanding of our Blessed Lady depends totally upon our understanding of her Son. Everything about her flows from her being Christ's mother; as our understanding of Him grows, our understanding of her grows. Unless we have some knowledge of the doctrines of Trinity and Incarnation, we can still love her but cannot know her; and we have already seen that loving without full knowledge is only a shadow of loving.

She is the Mother of God. The child she conceived and bore is God the Son. In His divine nature He had existed eternally. But His human nature He owed to her as much as any man owes his human nature to his mother. There is nothing that makes my mother mine which is lacking in her relation to Him as man. As God He was born of the Father before all ages; as man He was born at a particular moment in time of the Virgin Mary. Do not think it sufficient to call her the mother of His human nature: natures, we have already noted, do not have mothers. She was mother, as yours or mine is, of the person born of her. And the Person was God the Son.

It is a special mark of the Catholic as distinct from what we may call the typical Protestant that he finds this truth almost shattering in its greatness, its immensity; whereas to the other it is simply a biographical fact about Christ which one notes but does not linger upon. Naturally, he seems to say, if God was to become man, one would expect Him to have a mother; but having borne Him into the world, she had done her duty, and from now on our whole interest must be in Him, not her. When thought of at all, she must be thought of with respect. But she is not often thought of. Why should she be?

I have put this way of looking at her as a sort of rough outline of a whole state of mind. In its more extreme utterance it can be so comic that one almost forgets how tragic it is. On the outdoor platform I once had a questioner who said, solemnly, "I respect Christ's mother as I respect my own." The overwhelming temptation, when one hears such a remark, is to point to the difference between the two sons. But it is necessary to make clear why the difference makes a difference! We are not saying that mothers of holy children are better than mothers of less holy. The difference is not between one son who is holy and another who is less obviously so. It is between a son who is God and a son who is man only.

In seeing what the difference is, a good starting point is the simple fact that this Son existed before His mother. So that He is the only Son who was in a position to choose who His mother should be: He could choose therefore what every son would choose if He could, the mother who would suit him best. Further it goes with the very heart of sonship that a son wants to give his mother gifts; and Christ, being God, could give her all that she would want: to His giving power there was no limit. And what above all she wanted was union with God, the completest union possible to a human being of her will with God's will, grace therefore in her soul.

He was her Son, and He gave it lavishly. She responded totally, so that she was sinless. It was her response to the grace of God that made her supreme in holiness—higher even than the highest angel, the Church tells us. We may pause for a moment to look at this truth. By nature she was lower than the least angel, for human nature as such is less than angelic. But as we have already seen any relation in the order of grace is higher than any in the order of nature. It is by grace that we are closer to God; by our response, that is, to the created share in His own life that God offers us. By grace Our Lady outranks all created beings. But only because she responded more perfectly. Saint John Chrysostom says, "She would not have been blessed, though she had borne Him in the body, had she not heard the word of God and kept it."

Immaculate Conception and Assumption

We have considered one result of Our Lady's being the Mother of God—all sons want to give their mothers gifts, this Son could give without any limit save her power to receive; and what in supreme measure He gave was sanctifying grace. But there is one special element in His power to give that we might easily overlook. Because He was God, He could give His mother gifts not only before He was born of her, but before she was born herself! This is the meaning of the doctrine of the Immaculate Conception.

It is surprising how this phrase has caught the non-Catholic imagination, but more surprising how, for the non-Catholic who uses it, it has no trace of its true meaning. Ninety-nine times out of a hundred it is used as if it meant the Virgin birth of Christ. But it refers not to Christ's conception in Our Lady's womb, but to her conception in the womb of her own mother. It does not mean either that she was virginally conceived: she had a father and mother. It means that her Son's care for her and gifts to her began from the first moment of her existence.

For all of us conception comes when God creates a soul and unites it with the bodily element formed in the mother's womb. But from the very first moment of her soul's creation, it had, by God's gift, not natural life only but supernatural life. What this means quite simply is that she whom God chose to be His mother never existed for an instant without sanctifying grace in her soul.

A century ago the Church made this doctrine the subject of an infallible definition. For century upon century before that Catholics had held it for certain truth. Once the Church had formulated with all possible clearness the doctrines of the Trinity and Incarnation, so that Catholics could live day in and day out in the full awareness of who and what Christ is, they began to see it as unthinkable that He should have allowed His mother to exist for so much as an instant without sanctifying grace. Yet for many, devoted lovers of the Blessed Virgin, a troubling question remains. Our Lady had said in the Magnificat, "My spirit doth rejoice in God my Savior." How could God be her savior, what was there to save her from, if she had had grace always.

Gradually they came to see the answer, or rather the twofold answer. To save men from their sins is a great mercy of God; but to save this one woman from ever sinning was a greater mercy, but still a mercy. Not only that. Sinless as she was, possessed of grace at every instant, she was still member of a fallen race, a race to which heaven was closed. The Savior's redeeming act opened heaven to her as to all members of the race.

Roughly a hundred years after the definition of the Immaculate Conception came that of the Assumption of Our Blessed Lady. In the dogma, the word *assumption* has no relation to its ordinary English meaning of something one assumes because one cannot prove it. It means the taking of Our Lady, body and soul, into heaven. It is, if anything, earlier than the belief that she was conceived immaculate; and it is not too much to say that it never raised any serious doubt, or even problem, in the minds of Catholics.

It was an almost inevitable result of living with the full truth about her Son. For the ordinary man, there was the simple feeling that Christ would want His mother with Him in heaven, not her soul only but herself, body and soul. Any son would want that, and this was the one son who could have what He wanted! For the more instructed, probably, there was another element. It is a doctrine of the Church that all men would receive back the bodies from which their souls had been separated at death. The gap between was a result of sin, and Our Lady was sinless.

Men, of course, cannot pretend to know what God will or will not do. For all of us the temptation occasionally arises to decide some question with the confidence that the decision is God's, when all that we have done is to decide what we would do if we were God. But when the vast mass of Catholics see a conclusion as certain over a space of some fifteen hundred years, the risk is not great. It vanishes altogether when the Church gives its infallible definition.

Our Mother

At the Annunciation, theologians hold that with "be it done unto me according to thy word" Our Lady uttered the consent of the human race to the first step in its redemption. The Assumption means that in heaven she represents the human race redeemed: she alone is, body and soul, where all the saved will one day be. We must look a little more closely at her relation to the human race which at these two points she represents.

We call her our Mother, and for most of us the matter requires no discussion. Yet it repays discussion. If we take for granted that she is our Mother simply because she is Christ's, we omit something that matters for our understanding of what she means to us. As her Son, He drew His natural life from her; but, because He was her Redeemer, she drew her supernatural life from Him: and it is in the supernatural order, the order of grace, that she is our Mother.

How, in this order, does she become so? By her Son's appointment. In the Collect to her feast as Mediatrix of All Graces, the Church says it—"O Lord Jesus Christ, our Mediator with the Father, who hast deigned to appoint your most blessed Virgin Mother to be our Mother". The appointment was made upon Calvary. When Our Lord gave her the apostle John to be her son, He was not simply making provision for her. For that He had no need to wait for Calvary. Calvary was the sacrifice of the race's redemption; everything that He did and said on the Cross is related to that. So with His words to Our Lady and Saint John. It was as part of His plan of redemption that He was giving her to be the Mother of John—not of John as himself but as man. From that moment she is the Mother of us all.

What does motherhood carry with it? Essentially love and total willingness to serve. Those two things Catholics have always seen in her, telling her their needs with complete confidence, inwardly conversing with her freely. That is, we pray to her; which means that we ask her to pray for us—for all kinds of things, but especially for grace, which is what mattered most to her (matters most to us too though we do not always realize it). In the encyclical *Ad diem* Saint Pius X called her "the first steward in the dispensing of graces".

With this we come to an element in the redemption which we too easily fail to notice. Christ redeemed us, but it is in God's plan that the application to individual souls of the redemption Christ won should be by fellow members of the race: we are all called to be stewards in the dispensing of graces. The principal ways for every one of us are love, prayer, suffering.

None of these things would be of any effect if Christ had not died for us; but in union with His redemptive act they are of immense power. From the beginning of the Christian Church, their effect is taken for granted. Thus Saint Paul can tell his converts to pray for others *precisely because* there is one mediator between God and man (1 Tim 2:5). In other words, the fact that Our Lord is mediator does not make our prayer for one another unnecessary; it makes it effective.

Everyone's prayers can help others, but the holier, the more. With Christ and in Christ we are all called upon to take a part in redeeming others. All are meant to have a part in His redeeming work, but Mary above all; for she was sinless, she was wholly love, she suffered supremely.

The Mystical Body exists for the application of Christ's redemption to the souls of men; as I have said, we are all called upon to help in the application, but she is *the* Coredemptress. So that once again she represents the race, the redeemed race. So much of what we say when we speak of her and when we speak of the Church is interchangeable—we call her our Mother, for instance, and in the next breath we speak of our holy Mother the Church. The truth is that what the Church, the Mystical Body, does in its other members more or less well according to the individual's will to cooperate, she in her single person does continuously and perfectly. She is the *first* steward in the dispensing of graces.

XVI

GRACE, VIRTUES, GIFTS

By baptism we are incorporated with Christ, built into that Church which is truly His Body, so that we live in Him and He in us. We must look at this life, the life of grace, more closely. Reread Chapter IX on the Supernatural Life before continuing with what is here. What is said more lengthily there may be summarized briefly.

Men, we have seen, have by God's will a destiny of which by nature they are incapable; if we are to live the life of heaven, to see God directly, to "know as we are known", we have to receive new powers in our souls which are not there by nature. And, because this life is a preparation for the next, because the next life flows without break from this, we must receive these new powers in the soul here upon earth. As received here, the supernatural life, the life of sanctifying grace, does not produce its full flowering in giving us here and now the direct vision of God. But it does lift the soul to new possibilities even in this life.

Observe that we are not given a new soul, but new powers in the soul we already have. Our intellect is given a new access to truth by faith: now it can accept God as the supreme source of truth, whose word is final. The will receives two virtues. One is hope, by which it desires God in the certainty that He is attainable. The other is charity, by which it loves God. These three are called the theological virtues, because their object is God, they relate the soul directly and rightly to Him.

The Moral Virtues

With grace there enter the soul not only the theological virtues but also the moral virtues, which are concerned with our relation to all things less than God. Here too there is an uneven division between intellect and will, the intellect having one of them, prudence; the will having three, justice and temperance and fortitude.

Prudence first. It is possible for the intellect, enlightened by faith, to know the truth about God, yet fail to see all the windings of the road we must tread to come to Him and see how we should carry ourselves upon the road. Prudence is the virtue by which the grace-aided soul *sees* the world as it actually is and our relation to it as it should be. Unhappily prudence has, in ordinary speech, a meaning which can actually contradict the very nature of the virtue. It tends to mean something very close to timidity, playing everything safe, taking no risks—risks meaning anything that might reduce our material well-being—martyrdom, for instance. In fact there are circumstances in which letting oneself be martyred is highly prudent, and the avoidance of martyrdom imprudent in the extreme. There is no gain in avoiding martyrdom at the loss of one's eternal soul. The very motto of prudence is that he who loses his life shall save it.

Prudence is thus the virtue which enables the intellect to see what is right to do. The other three help the will to do what the intellect sees. Justice concerns our dealing with others. It is a burning will that they have what is due to them. It is not simply that we refrain from grasping what we are not entitled to; this of itself might be only spiritual anemia. Justice means a really profound concern that others should have their rights, driving us to do something about it!

Temperance and fortitude concern our handling of ourselves. The world contains things—in some moods we feel it is full of things—which attract us almost irresistibly—though we know we should not have them, cannot have them without damage to the soul. The world also contains things which frighten us, which we would do anything to avoid, yet which duty calls upon us to face. Temperance aids the will to turn from the dazzlingly attractive things we should shun. Fortitude aids the will to face what every instinct tells it to run away from. Temperance moderates us. Fortitude stimulates us.

With faith and hope and charity and the four moral virtues it might seem that we have all the helps the soul requires to reach its supernatural destiny. But there are more helps, as we shall see.

Actual Grace

So far all our talk has been of sanctifying grace. But there is actual grace too. The similarity of name, both being called grace, could mislead us into thinking they are practically identical. But the word *grace* simply means a free gift of God, something of which there is not even a beginning in our nature, wholly given therefore. But although both actual grace and sanctifying grace meet this definition, the gifts given in each are quite different. It might help our thinking if we spoke of one as supernatural life, the other as supernatural impulsion.

Sanctifying grace is a life in the soul, making it almost a new thing, giving it and its faculties new powers. Actual grace is the divine energy setting the soul in motion toward some particular goal otherwise beyond its reach. Sanctifying grace indwells the soul and abides in it. Actual grace does neither. It does not abide—it is transient, like a wind that blows for a while and then is gone, the whole point being to take advantage of it while it blows. Nor does it indwell: it does not live in the soul but acts upon it in a sense from outside; it sets intellect and will in motion without becoming a permanent quality of either, very much as a wind moves a boat but does not in any sense become a permanent element in the boat's structure.

We may indeed think of actual graces—observe that we never speak of sanctifying graces but only grace—as sudden gusts of the wind of the Spirit. To them applies very strongly what Our Lord said to Nicodemus (Jn 3:8): "The Spirit breathes where he will: and you hear his voice, but you know not whence he comes and whither he goes." Without this thrust of the divine energy, the soul could not take the first step in its sanctification. But with it, the soul is capable of movements otherwise beyond it. If it responds and makes them—above all a movement of love toward God—then it will receive sanctifying grace. If it responds, notice; for it is supernatural impulsion, not compulsion.

Actual graces do not cease when the soul receives sanctifying grace. God continues to send them to enable us in this, that or the other matter to see what is best for us to do and to make the effort, if we happen to be reluctant, to do it. This brings us to the gifts of the Holy Spirit. We receive these with sanctifying grace, so that they are abiding qualities in the graced soul. The simplest statement of their function is that they catch the wind of actual grace when it blows, so that we respond to it, and respond fruitfully.

The Gifts of the Holy Spirit

It is from Isaiah (11:2) that we get the names of the seven
gifts: he is speaking of the Messiah to come: "The Spirit
of the Lord shall rest upon him: the spirit of wisdom,
and of understanding, the spirit of counsel and of fortitude,
the spirit of knowledge and of piety. And he shall be filled
with the spirit of the fear of the Lord. He shall not judge
according to the sight of the eyes, nor approve according
to the hearing of the ears."

For once intellect gets more of them than will: to it
belong understanding, wisdom, knowledge, counsel. Each
of these is worth long and detailed study. Here we can
merely indicate what they are for. We have seen that by
the theological virtue of faith we accept whatever God has
revealed for no other reason than that He has revealed it;
by the gift of understanding we are aided to grasp more
clearly what the truths we have accepted actually mean,
and to go deeper and deeper in their exploration. We may
think of understanding as giving eyes to faith. Wisdom
makes the soul more intensely responsive not simply to
the meaning, but to the value of what we have learned
about God. Knowledge is also concerned with response to
value, but to the spiritual value of created things. Counsel
helps us to be aware of the special guidance offered us by
the Holy Spirit in relation to what we must do and must
avoid for our soul's eternal good here and now; in a way it
bears something of the same relation to the moral virtue of
prudence that understanding bears to faith.

There remain piety, fortitude and fear of the Lord. We
have seen how counsel gives a kind of special edge to
the moral virtue of prudence. These last three gifts bear
roughly the same relation to the other moral virtues.

Piety is related to justice in one rather special way. For, because justice means giving to others what they are entitled to, to it belongs the virtue of religion, which pays that debt to God. We may define piety as love of one to whom we are already bound by the duty of obedience. We may think of it as loving God solely because He is lovable—not because of the glory of the world He has created or because of all that He has done for ourselves, but simply for His own glory. It is a love of God, wholly self-forgetful.

Fortitude is related, naturally, to the virtue of the same name. Fear of the Lord is seen by theologians in special relation to the virtue of temperance. Temperance, remember, helps us to refuse delights forbidden by God's law; fear, the gift, aids in various ways but most, perhaps, by an awareness of the lovableness of God which does something to take the glow from the delight with which the forbidden action draws us.

In fact, the relation between the gifts and the virtues to which each brings what I have called edge, or impetus, or clarity is a matter upon which theologians have written profoundly and brilliantly, but it is rather beyond our present stage. But one thing at least we must add to this brief statement: just as in the giving of actual graces the Spirit blows where it pleases Him and we do not know whence or whither, or even with any certainty when, so the response within us of the gifts is something of which we are not normally aware. The supernatural life as a whole has no direct access to our bodily senses, or to the emotions, which lie in the frontier region where soul and body meet, or to our consciousness as it is aware of things in the natural order.

In our analysis of the life of grace we have talked of the seven virtues, theological and moral, and the seven gifts. Over and above these are the beatitudes and fruits which need not concern us now. All these, so to speak, *are* the state of grace; whoever is in it has them all—there is no such thing as being in grace and lacking any of them, though the dullness or reluctance of the response of our nature to one or other of them may make us feel that we do. With the first coming of grace to the soul we receive it totally. We may very well have increase of grace, but this will be a matter of growing intensity, not of new elements. The first coming is by faith, the root from which the whole life grows. Without it we should get none of the rest, for what sort of relation would we have with a God in whom we did not believe? It is worth dwelling on the simple fact that faith means a new contact of the intellect with God, and that it is in the direct contact of this same intellect with God that the Beatific Vision ultimately consists. Our end is in our beginning.

How Grace Is Lost

How do we lose grace? By mortal sin, obviously, a choice of our own will as against God's so serious and deliberate that it really breaks the union between us and Him. Here too we need a shade more precision. Think of grace under the figure of a tree—faith at the root, above it hope, above that charity, above that all the leaves and branches of moral virtues and gifts and beatitudes and fruits. Faith and hope and charity are the trunk of the tree. Each of these is lost by a serious sin against it; losing any one of them, we lose all of the tree above it, but not necessarily that which lies below. A sin against the love of God does not destroy hope or faith. These we lose only by sins which involve their direct denial. Hope is lost, as we have seen, by despair or presumption; faith by unbelief.

But charity is the life-giver. Sinning against it we lose the supernatural life, we are without sanctifying grace. We may still have faith and hope, and they will be quite real, but not saving, not life-giving—yet not valueless. They can be real aids to the movement of nature against sin which may lead God to energize once more in the soul by grace. A man who knows God attainable and desires to come to Him, though caught in some sin to which he is too powerfully attached, has a strong reason still for fighting against sin. Even if he has nothing left but faith—hope having gone the way of charity—yet the belief in God, though he is not doing anything about it, constitutes a point of return which the man without faith lacks; though even there we need place no limit to the life-giving power of the Holy Spirit—the prayers of others may still aid a man who will not pray for himself, winning actual graces to which man's power to respond does not cease while this life lasts.

XVII

THE SACRAMENTS

The Sacramental System

We receive grace by baptism. One who, through no fault of his own, is not baptized, may still receive it; for the Church teaches that everyone who reaches the use of reason is given by God sufficient actual grace to enable him, if he will, to lift his soul in a movement of love to God and so receive from God sanctifying grace. In Saint Augustine's words, "We are bound by the sacraments; God is not."

But baptism *is* God's plan for us. In form it is the pouring of water on the head, accompanied by the words, "I baptize thee in the name of the Father and of the Son and of the Holy Spirit." Its place in the giving of the new life was stated by Our Lord to Nicodemus: "Unless one be born again of water and the Holy Spirit, he shall not enter the kingdom of heaven." And Saint Paul told the Romans (6:3–7) "We were taken up into Christ by baptism ... in our baptism we have been buried with him, died like him, that so, just as Christ was raised up by his Father's power from the dead, we too might live and move in a new kind of existence."

One coming fresh to the idea might well feel a certain strangeness in baptism—a material thing, water, having this essential place in our reception of grace, which is wholly spiritual. Indeed there are spiritual men who reject it as a monstrous union of unrelated things, a profanation of the higher by the lower. In this they are forgetting themselves, I mean they are forgetting *themselves*, forgetting the persons that they are. If there are pure spirits—fallen angels—who also regard any union of matter and spirit as monstrous, they have a shade more excuse. For the men who thus reject it are themselves the result of a union of matter and spirit; grace is built into nature and our nature is like that. The union in man and the union in sacrament are both mysterious; but the same God who made the one made the other.

We have used the word *sacrament(s)* several times in the last few paragraphs. For baptism is the first of seven ways established by Christ for the use of material things to bring grace to souls. Sacrament is not only used for the first conveying of grace, but for many others, as we shall see. It is worth looking at the idea of sacrament more closely.

In two ways the sacramental system follows the same design as the nature into which grace is to be infused.

In the first place the materials used are water, bread, wine, oil and human speech. In a sense these five are a kind of skeleton upon which man's natural life is built; they are the basic elements, the first four making bodily life possible, the fifth being indispensable to social life. In the second place they are linked with what we may call the pattern or sequence or structure of human life in general. There is birth and growth and death; to these respond baptism, confirmation and extreme unction; in between comes the union of the sexes for the continuance of the race, to which corresponds matrimony; and for some the duty of representing God in relation to the community and the community in relation to God, for which Christ provided holy orders. Of these five sacraments, three—baptism, confirmation and holy orders—cannot be repeated at all, because, as Saint Thomas tells us, they represent ways of sharing in the priesthood of Christ. We shall return to this. Matrimony can be repeated, if a wife or husband dies; extreme unction can be repeated because it is given in danger of death, and although death comes only once, the danger of death may occur more frequently.

But there are two other elements, one essential to life and the other practically inseparable from it. One is the need for food, and the other the need for healing. These also have their corresponding sacrament. Penance is there, confession of sin to the priest followed by absolution, for healing; the Blessed Eucharist is there for the bread of our life.

A full treatment of the sacraments must come at a later stage of one's study of theology. Ideal for the purpose are the five volumes on the sacraments, written by Monsignor Pohle, translated by that wonderful lay theologian Arthur Preuss, published by Herder. Here we may at least glance at three major questions affecting them all—who administers, how they are administered, and what they do for us.

The Minister

Baptism is so vital—for it is the beginning of our life as members of Christ and one who has not received it can receive no other sacrament—that God allows *anyone* to baptize. Ideally, of course, it should be administered by a priest; but if necessary a layman can baptize; even one not himself baptized may do so, provided he means to do what the Church does.

We have touched upon the intention with which the one giving baptism gives it. It applies to all sacraments.

The minister is acting in the power of Christ; he is giving himself to be used by Christ—giving himself, note. Our Lord is not using him as a tool, for tools are simply used at the carpenter's will, their consent is not asked. The minister gives himself to be used as Christ wishes to use him—that, broadly, is the doctrine of intention.

There is one sacrament which cannot be administered by a priest at all—it is matrimony, for the man and woman to be married (provided they are baptized) administer it to each other. They must have their parish priest there, or another with his consent. If they live so far from a priest that it is practically impossible to have one present—a month's journey, for instance, or a desert island—then they may marry with no priest there.

The bishop confers holy orders, and normally confirmation, though he sometimes delegates one of his clergy. The other three—penance, Holy Eucharist, extreme unction—can be administered only by one who has received priestly orders.

How Administered

How the various sacraments are administered does not require detailed treatment in an elementary outline of theology. The Church speaks of the matter and form of each sacrament, and upon some points there is vast discussion among theologians. Here we need glance only at what must be *done* and what must be *said*.

Of baptism we have already spoken. In confirmation there is the laying on of the bishop's hands and the anointing of the forehead with consecrated oil.

Matrimony requires that the man and woman make announcement in the presence of witnesses of their wish to be husband and wife.

The person seeking the sacrament of penance must confess at least all mortal sins he has committed since he last received the sacrament, with contrition and the willingness to make whatever satisfaction is required. (Contrition and satisfaction will be explained later.) The priest must pronounce the words of absolution, "I absolve you from your sins."

Holy Eucharist requires that the priest say the words "This is my body" over wheaten bread, and the words "This is my blood" over wine of the grape. Theologians have much more to tell, but it need not be set out here.

In holy orders, the bishop lays his hands on the person to be ordained and says a prayer that he may receive the power of sacerdotal grace (the word *sacerdotal* comes from the Latin word for the offering of sacrifice).

In extreme unction the organs of sense are anointed with oil, and the priest prays for the forgiveness of sins committed through each of them (though a general prayer that the sick man's sins be forgiven has been held sufficient).

What has just been said of the necessary acts and words of the sacraments is the barest outline. There are further refinements as to what is needed for validity; and there are other requirements, not strictly essential for validity but called for by the Church's laws.

What the Sacraments Do

All the sacraments give sanctifying grace. Baptism initiates it; confession restores it when it is lost, or increases it if the penitent's sins are not mortal; the other sacraments all increase it. Each has its own special function as well. Here again only summaries are necessary at our present stage.

We have already spoken of confirmation as comparable with growing up. By it we become adult members of the Church. It brings the life of grace in us to maturity: it might be better to think of it as bringing us to maturity in the life of grace. By baptism, Saint Thomas says, we receive powers to do things which pertain to our own salvation; but in confirmation we receive power to do those things which belong to spiritual combat against the enemies of the Faith. We receive the power of confessing our Faith publicly and by words, as it were *ex officio*—that is, we have now not only the powers but an abiding right and duty to exercise them. We are not only members of the Church but soldiers, the Church's war is our affair.

Matrimony is—to some at least—the surprising sacrament: they had not expected that marriage, with the use of sex which is bound up with the primary reason for its existence as an institution, should be made a special way of receiving sanctifying grace. In fact, marriage is, supernaturally, in high honor. Saint Paul (Eph 5:23-30) compares the union of husband and wife with that of Christ and His Church. Once received, the sacrament of matrimony is continually operative while both partners live, giving special graces and aids where new situations arise and new difficulties call for them.

Extreme unction—the last anointing, which may not be the last, if the danger of death passes—is described in the Epistle of Saint James (5:14): "Is any man sick among you? Let him bring in the priests of the Church, and let them pray over him, anointing him with oil in the name of the Lord: and the prayer of faith shall save the sick man; and the Lord shall raise him up; and if he be in sins, they shall be forgiven him."

The Council of Trent calls anathema upon anyone who says that extreme unction "does not confer grace or remit sin or comfort the sick". Upon every phrase of this there is a great body of theological writing, beyond our present scope. At least we know with all confidence that there is increase of grace and strengthening of the soul for the trials inseparable from the approach of death; that sins are forgiven, even mortal, if there be no opportunity of the sacrament of penance; and that there may well be bodily healing if it be for the soul's good—if, for example, with longer life the soul might love and serve God better and grow in grace far beyond its present level.

With holy orders we come to the last of the three sacraments which can be conferred only once because they are ways of sharing in the priesthood of Christ. The first two are truly ways of sharing, but small ways compared with holy orders; for whereas baptism makes us members of the Body of the High Priest and confirmation gives us the duty and the power to serve the truths He revealed, holy orders makes a man a priest.

We have seen what sacraments he may administer; but two of the powers conferred upon him by the sacrament of holy orders are of supreme importance.

The first is that he can absolve from sin (though this power may be inoperative unless he also has jurisdiction, permission from the bishop of the diocese where he would use it: it is always operative if the penitent is dying).

The second is that he can offer the Sacrifice of the Mass; this power includes naturally the power to consecrate.

By penance sins are forgiven; the Blessed Eucharist strengthens our union with Christ by love and nourishes the soul. Both these sacraments are of such importance that we must proceed to look more closely at each of them.

Forgiveness of Sin

By the sins called "mortal"—death-bringing—we break the union of our will with God's and lose the supernatural life. There are lesser sins called "venial", which, because they are less serious or less deliberate, do not involve a rejection of God: they leave us with sanctifying grace still in our souls but they do weaken the nature in which grace is infused and thereby increase the danger of mortal sin.

It is not easy to find in Scripture a clear statement of the distinction between these two levels of sin—mainly because Scripture is almost wholly concerned with mortal sins. But the distinction is a plain matter of fact. In both we are breaking God's law, but the one breach involves rebellion and the other does not. There is something comparable in our relation to the law of the land. Aiding an enemy country in war breaks the law; so does driving beyond the speed limit. But one is treason, whereas many a man who would die for his country quite cheerfully does the other.

The sacrament of penance as the means of our obtaining forgiveness for sin was the first thing Our Lord established after His Resurrection, on the very day in fact. Having died to win redemption from sin, He makes immediate provision for the forgiveness of each individual's sins. Saint John (20:19–23) tells us how Christ came and stood in the midst of the apostles and said, "Peace be to you. As the Father hath sent me, I also send you." Then He breathed on them (only once before are we told of God breathing on man, at the very beginning, when He made man a living soul). And He said, "Receive ye the Holy Spirit: whose sins you shall forgive, they are forgiven them; and whose sins you shall retain, they are retained."

The Church, having thus received the power to forgive sins in Christ's name, has decided upon the way in which she shall exercise it: the Catholic confesses his sins to a priest. (Where individual confession is impossible— for example, when masses of men are exposed to immediate danger—the priest can absolve without it.) Sins thus confessed are under the seal—that is, the priest is strictly forbidden to mention them outside the confessional, even to the penitent himself—unless, of course, the penitent, seeking further advice, mentions them himself to the priest.

The first indispensable condition is that we be sorry for our sins. And not any kind of sorrow suffices; it must be sorrow for sin as an offense against God. What makes sin sin is not the damage, if any, done to others—which they might forgive us—but the disobedience of God's law. For that only God can forgive us; and our sorrow must be directed toward Him. Ideally it should be what is called "contrition"—sorrow for having disobeyed a good and loving God, to whom we owe all we have, who is entitled to our obedience. But provided we obey God's command to confess to His priest, a lesser sorrow than that may suffice—sorrow for having forfeited heaven and earned God's punishment. This is "attrition". By itself it would not suffice, but by the power of the sacrament it can.

To the non-Catholic, and even sometimes to the Catholic unnerved by the weight or number of his sins, the priest seems to have no obvious function, to be in fact an intruder in a matter that does not concern him. It is God, they argue, whose law is broken, God whose forgiveness we want; why not tell Him alone one's sorrow? How can we receive divine forgiveness from anyone but God?

For the Catholic, whatever his occasional wish that it should be otherwise, the matter is settled by the words of Christ already quoted—"whose sins you shall forgive, they are forgiven them." It is not for the sinner to decide how his sins shall be forgiven.

But the question is worth a longer look, for a profound principle is involved—God's plan of using men to convey His gifts to men. Life itself is from God, but He uses a human mother and father to give it to us. That, of course, is in the natural order. But it applies to the supernatural as well. His revelation normally comes to men through other men. The men who feel so certain that they must go to God alone for forgiveness would never know Christ lived, much less died for them, unless men had told them. It may have been living teachers if they belong to a teaching Church, or the long-dead men who wrote the Bible (to say nothing of the living men who gave it to them and told them what it was).

Of the whole of God's revelation this is true; new birth in baptism is given by God through man; so is Holy Communion (whatever the special value they attach to it). A reason, one imagines, for making this solitary exception of forgiveness for sin is that it involves confessing one's sins to a man, which naturally one dislikes.

In fact those who have practiced confession see certain high points of suitability in it: two, perhaps, especially.

The first is that it is a direct reversal of the process of sin. In sinning, the will chooses what pleases it, as against what God wills for it. In confessing, the will chooses what displeases it, because God wills that it should.

The second is that in it our sins, put into words weeks or months after we enjoyed them, look their worst. A glass of beer—to take a comparison outside the field of sin—can be a joy in the drinking. But leave the glass unwashed, and come upon it a month after—it will nauseate with its smell. Last month's sins, when we are forced really to look at them, take on their own natural stench.

Provided we are truly sorry and are willing to do whatever is in our power to undo any damage our sins have done to our victims—restoring money stolen, for instance, or retracting accusations we have falsely made against others—we receive absolution. The guilt of our sins is taken away. If our sorrow, though genuine and rightly motivated, has lacked the intensity called for by the sin's wickedness, there may still be punishment to make up for it; but the guilt is gone and the penance—suffered by us in this world or in purgatory—is measurable and will end. For those sins we have escaped the punishment that is eternal. What has already been referred to as satisfaction involves both repairing damage done to others and willingness to do the penance required.

But the great glory of the sacrament is not in the removal of guilt. The soul has been in the darkness of sin. The way to get rid of darkness is not to remove it in some suitable container, but to turn on the light. With confession and absolution, grace is restored to the soul. Once more we are supernaturally alive. As members of the Mystical Body we have been incorporated with Christ but His life has been blocked from our soul by unrepented sin. Now, once more, He is living in us.

XVIII

EUCHARIST AND MASS

The Real Presence

The Blessed Eucharist is *the* Sacrament. Baptism exists *for* it, all the others are enriched by it. The whole being is nourished by it. It is precisely food, which explains why it is the one sacrament that can be received daily. Without it, one petition in the *Our Father*—"Give us this day our daily bread"—lacks the fullness of its meaning.

Very early in His ministry, as Saint John tells us (Chapter 6), Our Lord gave the first promise of it. He had just worked what is probably the most famous of His miracles, the feeding of the five thousand. The next day, in the synagogue at Capernaum on the shore of the sea of Galilee, Our Lord made to them a speech which should be read and reread. Here we quote a few phrases: "I am the Bread of Life"; "I am the Living Bread, which came down from heaven. If any man eat of this bread, he shall live forever: and the bread that I will give, is my flesh for the life of the world"; "He that eats my flesh, and drinks my blood, has everlasting life: and I will raise him up on the Last Day. For my flesh is meat indeed: and my blood is drink indeed. He that eats my flesh, and drinks my blood, abides in me, and I in him"; "He that eats me shall live by me."

He saw that many of His own disciples were horrified at what He was saying. He went on: "It is the spirit that quickens: the flesh profits nothing." We know what He meant: in saying they must eat His flesh, He did not mean dead flesh but His body with the life in it, with the living soul in it. In some way He Himself, living, was to be the food of their soul's life. Needless to say, all this meant nothing whatever to those who heard it first. For many, it was the end of discipleship. They simply left Him, probably thinking that for a man to talk of giving them his flesh to eat was mere insanity. When He asked the apostles if they would go too, Peter gave Him one of the most moving answers in all man's history: "Lord, to whom shall we go?" He had not the faintest idea of what it all meant; but he had a total belief in the Master he had chosen and simply hoped that some day it would be made plain.

There is no hint that Our Lord ever raised the matter again until the Last Supper. Then His meaning was most marvelously made plain. What He said and did then is told us by Matthew, Mark and Luke; and Saint Paul tells it to the Corinthians (1 Cor 10—11). Saint John, who gives the longest account of the Last Supper, does not mention the institution of the Blessed Eucharist: his Gospel was written over thirty years after the others, to be read in a church which had been receiving Our Lord's Body and Blood for some sixty years. What he did provide is the account we have just been considering of Our Lord's first promise.

Here is Saint Matthew's account: "Jesus took bread, and blessed, and broke: and gave to His disciples, and said: Take ye and eat: This is My body. And taking the chalice He gave thanks: and gave to them, saying: Drink ye all of this. For this is My blood of the New Testament, which shall be shed for many unto remission of sins."

Since they deal with the food of our life, we must examine these words closely. What we are about to say of "This is My body" will do for "This is My blood" too. The word *is* need not detain us. There are those, bent upon escaping the plain meaning of the words used, who say that the phrase really means "This represents my body." This sounds very close to desperation. No competent speaker would ever talk like that, least of all Our Lord, least of all *then*. The word *this* deserves a closer look. Had He said "Here is My body", He might have meant that in some mysterious way, His body was there as well as, along with, the bread which seems so plainly to be there. But He said "*This* is My body"—this which I am holding, this which looks like bread but is not, this which was bread before I blessed it, this has become My body. Similarly this, which was wine, which still looks like wine, is not wine. It has become My blood.

Every life is nourished by its own kind—the body by material food, the intellect by mental food. But the life we are now concerned with is Christ living in us; the only possible food for it is Christ. So much is this so that in our own day you will scarcely find grace held to be Christ's life in us where the Eucharist is not held to be Christ Himself.

What Our Lord was giving us was a union with Himself closer than the apostles had in the three years of their companionship, than Mary Magdalen had when she clung to Him after His Resurrection. Two of Saint Paul's phrases, both from 1 Corinthians, Chapter 11, are specially worth noting: "Whosoever shall eat this bread, or drink the chalice of the Lord unworthily, shall be guilty of the Body and of the Blood of the Lord"; and "We, being many, are one bread, one body, all that partake of one bread"—a reminder that the Eucharist is not only for each man's soul but for the unity of the Mystical Body.

I can see why a Christian might be unable to bring Himself to believe it, finding it beyond his power to accept the idea that a man can give us his flesh to eat. But why should any man *want* to escape the plain meaning of the words?

For the Catholic nothing could be simpler. Whether he understands or not, he feels safe with Peter in the assurance that He who said He would give us His body to eat had the words of eternal life. Return again to what He said. The bread is not changed into the whole Christ, but into His Body; the wine is not changed into the whole Christ, but into His Blood. But Christ lives, death has no more dominion over Him. The bread becomes His Body, but where His Body is, there He is; the wine becomes His Blood but is not thereby separated from His Body, for that would mean death; where His Blood is, He is. Where either Body or Blood is, there is Christ, Body and Blood, soul and divinity. That is the doctrine of the Real Presence.

Transubstantiation

Besides the Real Presence which faith accepts and delights in, there is the doctrine of transubstantiation, from which we may at least get a glimpse of what happens when the priest consecrates bread and wine, so that they become Christ's Body and Christ's Blood.

At this stage, we must be content with only the simplest statement of the meaning of and distinction between substance and accidents, without which we should make nothing at all of transubstantiation. We shall concentrate upon bread, reminding ourselves once again that what is said applies in principle to wine as well.

We look at the bread the priest uses in the Sacrament. It is white, round, soft. The whiteness is not the bread, it is simply a quality that the bread has; the same is true of the roundness and the softness. There is something there that has these qualities, properties, attributes—the philosophers call all of them accidents. Whiteness and roundness we see; softness brings in the sense of touch. We might smell bread, and the smell of new bread is wonderful, but once again the smell is not the bread, but simply a property. The something which has the whiteness, the softness, the roundness, has the smell, and if we try another sense, the sense of taste, the same something has that special effect upon our palate.

In other words whatever the senses perceive—even with the aid of those instruments men are forever inventing to increase the reach of the senses—is always of this same sort, a quality, a property, an attribute; no sense perceives the something which *has* all these qualities. This something is what the philosophers call substance; the rest are accidents which it possesses. Our senses perceive accidents; only the mind knows the substance. This is true of bread, it is true of every created thing. Left to itself, the mind assumes that the substance is that which, in all its past experience, has been found to have that particular group of accidents. But in these two instances, the bread and wine of the Eucharist, the mind is not left to itself. By the revelation of Christ it knows that the substance has been changed, in the one case into the substance of His Body, in the other into the substance of His Blood.

The senses can no more perceive the new substance resulting from the Consecration than they could have perceived the substance there before. We cannot repeat too often that senses can perceive only accidents, and Consecration changes only the substance. The accidents remain in their totality—for example, that which was wine and is now Christ's blood still has the smell of wine, the intoxicating power of wine. One is occasionally startled to find some scientist claiming to have put all the resources of his laboratory into testing the consecrated bread; he announces triumphantly that there is no change whatever, no difference between this and any other bread. We could have told him that, without the aid of any instrument. For all that instruments can do is to make contact with the accidents, and it is part of the doctrine of transubstantiation that the accidents undergo no change whatever. If our scientist had announced that he *had* found a change, that would be really startling and upsetting.

The accidents, then, remain; but not, of course, as accidents of Christ's body. It is not His body which has the whiteness and the roundness and the softness. The accidents once held in existence by the substance of bread, and those others once held in existence by the substance of wine, are now held in existence solely by God's will to maintain them.

What of Christ's Body, now sacramentally present? We must leave the philosophy of this for a later stage in our study. All we shall say here is that His body is wholly present, though not (as Saint Thomas among others tells us) extended in space. One further element in the doctrine of the Real Presence needs to be stated—Christ's body remains in the communicant as long as the accidents remain themselves. Where, in the normal action of our bodily processes, they are so changed as to be no longer accidents of bread or accidents of wine, Christ's Real Presence in us ceases.

This very sketchy outline of the doctrine of transubstantiation is almost pathetic. But like so much in this book, what is here is only a beginning; you have the rest of life before you!

Communion in One Kind

Ordinarily, the Catholic receives Communion under the form of bread only—what is called Communion in one kind. He does not feel cheated thereby. Receiving Our Lord's Body, we do, as we have seen, receive the Blood, for they are inseparable; we receive Our Lord Himself whole and entire, for He is living now and eternally. Yet we may still have an uneasy feeling that after all, at the Last Supper, Our Lord established Communion in both kinds, and commanded both to the first men who received it.

Communion in both kinds has been administered to the laity by the Church at various ages in the past, and indeed is administered now to Catholics of the various Uniate rites. But in the Latin rite, it has long been given to the laity under the form of bread only [Sheed writes in 1957]. The simple reason is that we were not at the Last Supper! It was precisely to the apostles as the first priests of His Church that He gave commandment at the Last Supper. After He had given them His Body to eat and His Blood to drink, He added, as Saint Paul tells us (1 Cor 11:24 and 25) "This do for the commemoration of me." In other words, He was speaking to the men who should do throughout the ages what He had just done—consecrate bread and wine so that they might become His Body and Blood.

We of the laity receive Communion because Our Lord commanded, long before in Galilee, that we should receive His Body and Blood, and receiving either, we receive both. It is the priest offering the Sacrifice who consecrates in both kinds, and receives in both kinds—even a priest, going up to the altar rail at another priest's Mass, receives under the form of bread only. The twofold Consecration, which naturally involves the twofold reception, belongs to the offering of the Sacrifice of the Mass.

The Sacrifice of the Mass

Upon Calvary Christ Our Lord offered Himself in sacrifice for the redemption of the human race. There had been sacrifices before Calvary, myriads of them—foreshadowings, figures, distortions often enough, but reaching out strongly or feebly toward the perfection of Calvary's sacrifice.

They represented an awareness in men, a sort of instinct, that they must from time to time take something out of that vast store of things God had given them and give it back to Him. Men might have used the thing for themselves but chose not to: they offered it to God, made it sacred (that is what the word *sacrifice* means). In itself, sacrifice is simply the admission that all things are God's; even in a sinless world this would be true, and men would want to utter the truth by sacrifice. With sin, there was a new element: sacrifice would include the destruction of the thing offered—an animal, usually.

We can study these sacrifices, as they were before Calvary at once perfected and ended them, in the Temple sacrifices of the Jews, the Chosen People. The whole air of the Old Testament is heavy with the odor of animals slain and offered to God. The slaying and the offering—immolation and oblation—were both necessary elements. But whereas the offering was always made by the priests, the slaying need not be done by them; often it was the work of the Temple servants. For it was not the slaying that made the object sacred, but the offering. The essential thing was that the priest offer a living thing slain.

With Christ, we have said, sacrifice came to its perfection. The priest was perfect, for Christ was the priest. The victim was perfect, for He was the victim too. He offered Himself, slain. But not slain by Himself. He was slain by others, slain indeed by His enemies.

What He did was complete, once for all, not to be repeated. It accomplished three things principally—atoned for the sin of the race, healed the breach between the race and God, opened heaven to men, opened it never to be closed. He is "the propitiation for our sins, and not for ours only but for those of the whole world" (1 Jn 2:1).

With such completion, what was still to be done? For something *was* still to be done. Christ is still in action on men's behalf, as the Epistle to the Hebrews tells us. Jesus has entered "into heaven itself, that He may appear *now*, in the presence of God for us" (9:24). He is "always living to make intercession for us" (7:25). We have the answer to what still remains to be done: no addition to what was done on Calvary, but its application to each man—that each of us should receive for himself what Our Lord won for the race.

The "intercession" just spoken of is, need we say, no new sacrifice but the showing to God of the sacrifice of Calvary. The Victim, once slain, now deathless, stands before God, with the marks of the slaying still upon Him—"a Lamb standing, *as it were* slain" (Rev 5:6).

We are now in a better position to understand the Sacrifice of the Mass. In heaven Christ is presenting Himself, once slain upon Calvary, to His heavenly Father. On earth the priest—by Christ's command, in Christ's name, by Christ's power—is offering to God the Victim once slain upon Calvary. Nor does this mean a new sacrifice, but Calvary's sacrifice presented anew—in order that the redemption won for our race should produce its fruit in us individually.

In the Mass the priest consecrates bread and wine, so that they become Christ's Body and Blood. Thus the Christ he offers is truly there, really there. The Church sees the separate Consecration as belonging to the very essence of the Mass. It is a reminder of Christ's death—and He had told His first priests at the Last Supper that, in doing what He had just done, "they should show forth the death of the Lord, until He comes" (1 Cor 11:26). They should *show forth* Christ's death, remind us of His death, not, of course, kill Him: any more than He had killed Himself on Calvary.

The priest offers the sacrifice. But we are, in our lesser way, offerers too. Twice we are told so in the Ordinary of the Mass. When the priest turns to the congregation at the Orate Fratres, he says to them, "Pray, brethren, that my sacrifice *and yours* should be acceptable to God the Father Almighty." After the Consecration he says, "we thy servants and also thy holy people (*plebs tua sancta*) ... offer ... a pure, holy and immaculate Victim." To see ourselves merely as spectators at Mass is to miss the opportunity to take our part in the highest action done upon earth.

One element in the Mass remains to be mentioned. We, united with Christ's priests, have offered Our Lord to God. And God gives Him back to us, to be the life of our life. That is what Holy Communion means. God, while retaining Christ for His own, also shares Him with us. So that God and man, each in His own way, receive the slain and risen God-man.

XIX

THE NEXT LIFE

Death

For every man the moment comes when the body has been so weakened or damaged that it can no longer respond to the life-giving energies pouring into it from the soul. This is the moment of death. The body proceeds to dissolve. What of the soul?

The soul, remember, did not receive its existence from the body; each soul is created directly by God.

The soul did not begin from the body; there is no reason why it should end with it. And once we have grasped that the soul is a spirit, and realize what a spirit is, we know that it cannot end. We are so accustomed to the union of soul and body that it is easy to feel that neither can exist, still less function, without the other. In the conditions of this life, the mind gets knowledge by its action upon the information brought to it by the body's senses, and we feel that it would be helpless without them.

But closer consideration shows that the real strangeness lies not in the soul's separation from the body but in the use the soul makes of the body while their union lasts. That a spirit, whose very nature is to know, should be dependent in its knowing upon a material body, which itself knows nothing, is sufficiently mysterious. We do not know *how* the spirit takes over the information brought by the senses, only that in the conditions of this life it does. Nothing entitles us to hold that in the totally different conditions of the next life it still must.

The philosophers will carry you further. Meanwhile let us concentrate upon what God has told us of what follows the separation of soul and body.

It could hardly be put more neatly than by a song of a century back:

> "John Brown's body lies a-moldering in the grave,
> His soul is marching on!"

Marching on to what? Go back a further half-century to Coleridge's "Ancient Mariner":

> "The souls did from their bodies fly—
> They fled to bliss or woe."

Bliss or woe—what decides?

Where the soul goes at death is decided by what we love. There is a marvelous phrase of Saint Augustine— "*amor meus pondus meum*"—my love is my weight. In material things he saw weight deciding their movement— the heavy things went downward, the lighter upward. In the person, love does the same. He continues with a phrase roughly translatable as "wherever it is that I go, my love is what takes me there." One remembers Scripture's grim phrase about dead Judas—"he went to his own place." His love bore him there, his love for Judas.

For by the end of life the will has made its choice. Our love is either for God, or for self as distinct from God. Love of God takes us to God. Love of self as distinct from God takes us to a separation of self from God. Our Lord

(Mt 25:41) condenses the reality of hell into two elements—departure from God, everlasting fire.

Hell

There is a horror in the thought of hell which, unless we use our mind fully upon what it means, can bring a taint, a perversion, into our comprehension of God. It can in plain words damage or destroy our grasp of the supreme truth about God uttered by the beloved disciple—"God is love." The perversion can take two forms.

The commonest is the feeling that hell and a loving God cannot be reconciled; if hell exists God is not love or, alternatively, since God is love, hell cannot exist.

Less common, subtler, but if anything more dangerous is one that can be found among many devoted Christians—a whole-hearted acceptance of hell, an almost luscious delight in the invention of tortures to be inflicted by a raging God upon sinners (in whose number they themselves evidently are not). They will associate this with God's love, but in such a way that love has a meaning unrelated to any known among men.

They tell a story in Scotland of a preacher describing the sufferings of the damned: these are up to their necks in boiling pitch; suddenly an angel swoops down with a scythe; they bury their heads in the pitch, emerge with their eyes streaming and gasp (I spare you the Scottish accent): "But, Lord, we didn't know." Then the Lord, bending over them "with infinite mercy and compassion", said, "Well, you know now."

It is a jest, of course, an exaggeration. But the exaggeration is not wholly wild, and there is a streak of seriousness in the jest. It would be no gain to be right about hell and wrong about God. We must see both truths—hell's existence and God's love—together.

The first perversion—that hell is incapable of reconciliation with love—is shown to be such by the single fact that hell's existence is taught us by Christ who was supremely love. We have referred to one phrase. Earlier in Saint Matthew's Gospel comes the Sermon on the Mount which begins with the Beatitudes and continues through three chapters (5–8). In it Our Lord warns His hearers of hell at least five times. He speaks of it seriously but not, to use our earlier word, lusciously. We must study it seriously.

Leaving aside fancy—especially the sort of lavish indulgence in the invention of horrors that Dante goes in for—what do we actually know about hell? That it exists; that it came into existence with the fall of Satan and the angels who joined him in rebellion; that it is a place of suffering; that it is eternal. Of details, we have the one word *fire*, used of it more than once by Our Lord. It clearly means great suffering, for there are not many sufferings possible on earth worse than fire can inflict. But it does not help us much as detail; it differs too much from the fire we know: since it torments spirits (souls separated from bodies at death, angels who have never had bodies), and it does not consume bodies (when these are rejoined to souls at the end of the world).

Approach it as profound mystery—the mystery not of God's cruelty but of man's power to hate God. I do not mean that in most sinners hatred of God is primary or that sin begins with it. Sin begins with a perverted love of self. But love of self can grow monstrous, a sort of idolization of self, crowding out the love of all else and capable of turning into hatred of God. That may occur in this life or at death: to self-love grown monstrous God will be hateful once He is seen as the rival to the adored self.

The man, then, has chosen separation from God. The principal pain of hell results inevitably from the separation. Theologians call it the pain of loss. We were all made by God for union with Himself. Every one of us is a mass of needs which only God can meet. It is no exaggeration to say that the soul needs God as the body needs food or water. To be deprived of these means agony, fearful while it lasts; but it will end in death. There is a like agony of unmet need for the soul deprived of God; and it will not end in death, for the soul is a spirit.

The lost soul has chosen self-sufficiency, and it is not sufficient. It has made itself its god, and a pitifully, desperately needy god it proves. This is the deepest torment of hell. What punishment the divine Justice may inflict, we do not know. Theologians, seeing the pain of loss primary, speak also of the pain of sense. This may very well include punishment, and must in any event include sufferings of soul, and ultimately body, from the loss not only of God but of so much besides—the love and fellowship of other men and women, for example.

But being deprived of God is the essential pain, and this deprivation is willed by the self. It has nothing of God but His will to maintain it in existence. The God who alone could nourish it, it will not have.

When a man dies loving self to the hatred of God, what can God do with him? What He does do we know on His own word—He lets him go to his own place. It is hard to see what else He could do. He can hardly take him into heaven, for that would mean an inconceivably close union with the God he hates, a ceaseless torment to the self he loves. Those who deny the existence of hell so confidently never seem to have considered this problem of the people who have made the choice of self against God (though there is nothing in our experience of life to make us feel it impossible). When their attention is drawn to it, they still do not consider it: they merely rap out the suggestion that God should simply annihilate such people—before birth perhaps, by withholding existence from those He knew would make the choice of hatred. A study of the reasons God may have for not annihilating those who hate Him would take us theologically very deep. But quite apart from these, we have no reason of our own to conclude that condemned souls would want annihilation. To me it seems at least probable that love of self carried to that intensity would involve a clinging to self at all costs.

Purgatory

It is with some relief that we turn to the other possible love. At the end of life the will may have chosen to love God. As we have seen, the love of God will take the soul to God. The God-loving soul too will go to its own place, and its place is the presence of God.

In simple words, the soul is in sanctifying grace, whose very life principle is charity, whose one purpose in the design of God is to bring men to the Beatific Vision. Yet it is possible for the soul, even supernaturalized by grace, to love God, yet not wholly. Its love of God is the decisive element in it, yet there may be lightless, lifeless elements in the way of that love's totality. There may be small things, unimportant things that we cling to, which are not according to God's will; along with the upward flight there may linger a certain downdrag to self, which may be no great matter yet *is* a defect in love, a defilement of love's purity. We learn from Revelation (21:27) that nothing defiled can enter heaven.

We might feel that faults so trifling might simply be overlooked by God, but He knows that perfection is, Himself aiding, within our grasp and He has given us the command: "Be ye also perfect, as my heavenly Father is perfect."

For most of us it is a plain matter of experience that our life is like that. We may really love God and try hard to serve Him. Yet we are conscious of venial sins, committed in the past and not repented, liable to be committed in the future; we are conscious also, if we really think about it, of mortal sins repented yet not with the intensity that their foulness calls for; we feel that there are tendencies unconquered in us that could lead again, as so often in the past, to mortal sin. We make continuing efforts at improvement, but can hardly convince ourselves that we have tried our hardest. The state I have described is that in which a great many people live. The possibility is that in that state many will be found by death.

We may well believe that there are special aids at death. The prayers of others can bring actual graces. Extreme unction, the last anointing, can cleanse us wholly—yet even that sacrament we can keep from complete fullness by some defect in the disposition with which we receive it. We may leave this life loving God, yet not perfect, not undefiled.

Observe that things of the kind I have listed are defects in nature, elements preventing total harmony between our nature and the supernature that has been infused into it. We love God, and there is no abiding place for love of God save the presence of God. But for that place we are still not ready. Purgatory exists to make us ready. The word is from a Latin verb meaning to cleanse; and cleansing is precisely what purgatory is for. We gain no grace there, we emerge from purgatory with no increase of supernatural life. It exists solely for the cleansing of our nature.

At this point one may suddenly remember Saint John's phrase, "The blood of Christ cleanses us from all iniquity"

(1 Jn 1:7). We may find ourselves wondering, if Christ's blood cleanses us from all iniquity, what there is left for purgatory to cleanse us from. It is worth following up our wonder. It is true that nothing whatever can be cleansed in us apart from Christ's sacrifice on Calvary. Yet men may fail, totally or partially, to be cleansed by it. There is a part that they themselves must play if Christ's blood is to do that cleansing which it alone can do. It is with this part that purgatory is concerned. It may seem like laboring a truth already made sufficiently obvious to say that purgatory does nothing for us that Christ's blood alone can do; it simply removes the obstacles that we have interposed to the cleansing power of His blood.

Far from being a lessening of Calvary's power, the existence of purgatory means that this power can reach beyond the grave. If there is any spark of the supernatural life in us, however overlaid by natural grossness, Our Lord's blood can still remove the grossness, and the supernatural life can at last reach its own true end.

How are the defects of nature removed in purgatory? By direct action upon them, the most direct action possible, namely suffering. Twice before in this book we have dwelt upon what we may call the organic connection between accepted suffering and healing; we have seen that suffering of this kind is not the vengeance of an angry Judge, but the remedy of a Physician who understands us perfectly. We see the same truth in operation in purgatory. Of the nature of the suffering, we have no revelation. But two elements in it seem obvious enough. The first is the soul's realization, surpassing any that could possibly be had in this life, of the evil of even venial sin, still more of the mortal sins which in this life it repented but not sufficiently. The second is the soul's longing for the vision of God, which it may not yet have.

But, as we have already shown, the acceptance of suffering is a reversal of the process of sin. For sin is the thrust
of one's own will against God's. The total acceptance of
God's will at whatever cost to the self brings sure healing.
One final matter seems worth mentioning. The Church
teaches us that souls in purgatory may be speeded toward
healing, and so toward entry into heaven, by the prayers
of us who remain upon earth. There is a special joy for
the Catholic in praying for his dead, if only in the feeling
that there is still something he can do for people he loved
upon earth.

Heaven

When the downdrag to self has all gone, whether at the
moment of death or after the suffering of purgatory, the
soul speeds to God. It attains that total union with God for
which He created all men.

At this point, what is said of the Beatific Vision in chapter nine should be read again carefully. Observe how the
very heart of life in heaven is expressed in *seeing*. Our Lord
says that the guardian angels "see the face of my Father
continually"; Saint Paul says that in heaven we shall "know
as we are known", shall "see face to face". Saint John says
"we shall see Him as He is."

Just as the knowledge of God by faith is the root of the
supernatural life here below, the knowledge of God by
sight is its very essence in heaven. Everything else flows
from that. The Church has worked out in careful detail
the meaning of this seeing. Thus Benedict XII tells us
that the souls in heaven "see the divine essence with an
intuitive face-to-face vision". All the great theologians
have worked upon the distinction between the intellect's

natural knowledge by way of idea and the direct vision of God in heaven—God Himself taking the place of the idea of God.

We shall see God as He is, see Father, Son and Holy Spirit in the distinctness of persons. Mystery there will still be, for we shall remain finite, limited, and the finite mind cannot wholly contain the Infinite God. But the Mystery, too, will be a cause of bliss.

The contact of the intellect with God means, of course, contact of the whole soul. The intellect, as we have seen, is not simply a part of the soul, which might be in direct contact with God leaving other parts of the soul out of contact. The soul has no parts; it is, in the sense we have explained, simple. The will too is in direct contact with God, loving Him with nothing between; and this is true of the whole of man's being.

Every power in us, in fact, will be working at the fullness of intensity upon God who is the fullness of Reality. Here we have the very heart of happiness.

In this contact, the soul does not cease to be itself, but is more wholly itself than it has ever been. It is not merged in God, like a drop lost in the bucket of the infinite. The Infinite, one need hardly say at this stage, is not a bucket; the Infinite too is wholly simple and cannot receive admixture. God will always be Himself, man will always be himself, always God's image. Nor, remaining eternally distinct from God, does man, as some pious writers seem to suggest, lose all consciousness of self. One assumes that, thus writing, they intentionally exaggerate, their object being to emphasize the glory of the Infinite. But every man is the work of God, and God's glory is not served by ignoring any part of His work, even the part that happens to be oneself. God still deserves praise for having created us of nothing, still deserves gratitude;

to lose all consciousness of self is no good basis for praise or thanksgiving.

There is another result of the desire to glorify God. We must be gratefully and delightedly conscious not only of ourselves but of all the other souls in heaven who are of God's workmanship. He loves them, they are united with Him; we must love them and be in the closest union with them.

Of those we shall thus know and love as we have never known or loved anyone on earth, the first is evidently Christ, God the Son in His human nature, and the second, as evidently, His Mother. These two alone, before the Last Judgment and the end of the world, will have their risen bodies. There will be other human souls; there will be the angels.

Our love for those still upon earth will not have perished; love is not meant to perish. So far as God reveals their condition to us, we shall be profoundly concerned, and shall pray God to aid them. If the objection is raised that all this concern with other people seems to involve too much distraction from the direct vision of God, Our Lord Himself has answered it. For it was of the angels entrusted with the guardianship of small children here upon earth that He said, "They see the face of my Father continually."

For many, most of us perhaps, the first reaction to a straightforward statement of this sort about heaven is a feeling that there seem to be a lot of earthly pleasures we shall miss rather badly. We imagine ourselves sometimes looking back to the dear dead days before we were raised to eternal bliss.

Two immediate considerations follow this. The more obvious is that we have no awareness of what the *pleasure* of life in heaven will be. There is no way of realizing a

pleasure until one has enjoyed it. The most eloquent analysis will not tell one with no experience of it. You cannot
convey the delight of color to a blind man. There are a
host of adult joys that cannot be conveyed to children. In
heaven the blindness of earth will be gone; we shall at last
be grown-up.

The other consideration is that we have taken pleasure
in things or happenings in this life either for the reality in
them or for what we delude ourselves into imagining that
they possess. The second sort will cease in heaven, for
there is no place for delusion or illusion there. But the first
sort we shall have in greater measure, because whatever
reality is in any created thing is there by the gift of God.
It is therefore, in infinite perfection, in God Himself, and
with Him we shall be in living contact.

XX

THE END OF THE WORLD

Does the soul in heaven miss the body it once had? Without sorrow, yes. It knows the powers in itself for the animation of a material body which are the very reason for this one spirit's existing *as* a soul. Knowing the powers, it must know the joy it will be to have them once more in exercise.

When the world ends, all human souls, saved or lost, will be reunited with their bodies. Both of the world's end and the state of the risen bodies we have been given some glimpses.

The world will end when some goal has been attained by the human race. It is mere folly to think of God suddenly losing patience, feeling that the whole chaotic business has gone on long enough and deciding to end the world there and then. God, who knows all things eternally, has no such new decision to make, sudden or otherwise. God, creating the world, knew its ending.

The goal seems clearly to be the completion of the Mystical Body—when it shall have reached "perfect manhood, that maturity which is proportioned to the completed growth of Christ". As we have seen, the Mystical Body is not simply a spiritual replica of our natural body. What its maturity, its completion will be, we do not know. God knows. When all who are to be incorporated in it are incorporated, the human race will have achieved its highest triumph; there will be no point or even meaning in bringing new men into existence. This world will end.

Of the signs that the end is approaching Scripture speaks many times, but it is not always easy to understand what it says. There will be a vast Apostasy. Antichrist will come—a man, not a demon, for "he shall make no account of the god of his fathers" (Dan 11), but Satan will aid him (2 Thess 2); he will have the "false prophet" as his chief minister. Once at least Saint Paul mentions the conversion of the Jewish people as a whole. There is a great deal of literature—ranging between pure theology and sheer delirium—upon these points, for they have fascinated Christians.

What is told us clearly is that Christ will return in power and majesty to judge all men, the living and the dead; the bodies of the dead will have risen and all men will once more be that union of spirit and matter which constitutes them fully as men. Then each man will see, not only his own individual destiny, but the shape and bearing of humanity's history as a whole.

What the resurrection of the body will mean to the lost, we have no way of knowing. But we can see one fact about what it will mean to the saved. At last they will know what it is to be a man—not a mess, as so many of us are for so much of our lives. Nor is it only to the worst, the messes among us, that the experience of total manhood, integral manhood, will come new. Even the holiest have not known in their earthly life the complete subjection of body to soul in which alone the body is made glorious. They have, some few of them perhaps, reached the point where the soul is free from that subjection to the body which came with sin.

But for all men in heaven the condition first planned by God will have been restored. The soul is completely obedient to God (in an ecstasy of union that unfallen Adam never knew), the body, now glorified, is completely obedient to the soul. It does not hinder the soul by providing competing pleasures; it responds perfectly to the soul's animating energies; it does not limit the soul; it is wholly for the soul's use. Even the saints have not experienced that.

Earth and sky will end; but there will be a new sky and a new earth: so we read in Chapter 21 of Revelation. The whole chapter is well worth reading. Here is its opening:

> "Then I saw a new heaven, and a new earth. The old heaven, the old earth had vanished, and there was no more sea. And I, John, saw in my vision that holy city which is the new Jerusalem.... I heard, too, a voice which cried aloud from the throne, Here is God's tabernacle pitched among men; He will dwell with them, and they will be His own people.... He will wipe away every tear from their eyes, and there will be no more death, or mourning."

EPILOGUE

From a speech given by the author at the Second World Congress for the Lay Apostolate (October 1957, Rome)

The Layman in the Church

I

By confirmation, the layman is *miles* of the Church Militant. The Church on earth is at war, an army therefore. Its officers are the clergy, we are the rank and file, the simple soldiery—what in the British Army would be called privates, in the American Army enlisted men or G.I.'s. We must consider our part in the warfare.

To begin with we must understand what the warfare is. It is being fought not simply to enlarge the Church, but to bring souls into union with Christ. It is that strangest of wars which is fought *for* the enemy, not against him. Even the term enemy must not be allowed to mislead.

Every unbeliever is, as every Catholic is, a being with an immortal spirit, made in the image of God, for whom Christ died. However violently hostile to the Church or to Christ he may be, our aim is to convert him, not simply to defeat him, still less to destroy him. We must never forget that the Devil wants his soul in hell as he wants ours, and we must fight the Devil for him. We may be forced to oppose a man to prevent his endangering souls; but always we want to win him, for his own soul's salvation. It is in the power of the Holy Spirit that we must fight, and He is the Love of the Father and the Son; insofar as the Church's soldiers fight in hatred, they are fighting against Him.

The war is fought with many weapons, but the principal one is truth. For truth means seeing reality as it is. Men who do not know what God is, what man's soul is, what the purpose of life is and what follows death, are simply not living in the real world. And this is the condition of the great mass of the human race. They need to be shown the truths about God, the spiritual order, the world to come, for men cannot live according to a reality which they do not see—nor dare we blame them for failing to live according to a reality which we have never shown them. Above all they must come to see and know Christ Our Lord, in whom all truth is contained and by whom it is announced to men.

Who is to show them these truths?

Here we must dwell for a moment upon a simple fact. We are living in a noisy world, never has it been so filled with clamor. The radio is turned on all the time and so is television; there are cinemas, sporting events, mass-circulation magazines and a flood of daily papers; motor cars are rushing about the roads and airplanes about the sky. In all this uproar, how is truth to be heard, revealed truth? We have a great Pope, who utters truth profoundly, but the great mass of people never hear what he says, simply *cannot* hear what he says. So it is with our bishops, our great preachers and writers—their voices can reach only a small minority, for the rest they are lost in the whirlwind.

There is only one voice that can be heard, the voice of a man speaking to his friend—speaking to the man next door, the man he works with, plays with, travels with. That voice, and only that, can secure attention. Therefore it is upon that voice that the winning of the war in our time and place depends. The clergy must teach us of the laity, unless we learn from them there is only loss for us too; but the laity must convey the message one by one, to unbelievers one by one. Meetings have their part, and there should be more of them; but the daily, hourly fighting of the war is only possible if each Catholic is equipped to lead toward the truth the people he personally meets.

For this the layman must be equipped, above all with the truths about God and the soul and the next life and Christ Our Lord. It is not necessary that he should be trained in argument, able to prove the existence of God, for instance, or the spirituality of the soul. What is essential is that he know what the truths themselves mean, and what difference they make; and not only know these things, but be able to utter them.

Without utterance, truth lies mute within us, helping no one but our own self. We first learn the doctrines, then we start all over again to learn to say them; for there is a great gap between the seeing and the saying of spiritual realities. We must above all study the mind to which the doctrines must be offered—what it already contains and what it lacks, how it works, the words it knows.

But the mode of utterance is not the immediate problem: too many laymen do not know these great truths well enough to utter them even badly. They know, or at least they have been taught, the wonderful formulas of the Catechism in which the truths are enshrined, but they do not grasp what the formulas are actually saying; therefore they cannot possibly so present them that another man will be won to see their beauty, still less the difference it would make to his own life if he accepted them.

Consider the grasp of the average layman, not specially instructed, upon the doctrine of the Blessed Trinity. He knows that there are three Persons in one God, and that the Persons are called Father, Son and Holy Spirit. But that is almost all he does know, certainly that is all he can put into words. Whenever he goes beyond that, he makes the theologian writhe. How often one has heard lay people say, "The poor Holy Spirit, we neglect Him so!" In other words, the Holy Spirit is being pitied because *we* do not give Him sufficient of our attention, so that He must simply put up with the company of the Father and the Son.

This, you say, is frantic nonsense, only to be heard upon the lips of the very uninstructed Catholic. But the uninstructed Catholic is frequently a person of good secular education. One has met Catholic university professors.... It was a very important Catholic layman indeed who, being asked how could God be in three Persons, answered, "God is omnipotent and can be in as many persons as He pleases." As a member of the Catholic Evidence Guild, which conducts outdoor meetings in Hyde Park and all over England, I am one of those who examine great numbers of lay people who join the Guild in order to be trained for its work. I record a dialogue which I have heard frequently.

The trainee is asked if God died on the Cross. He instantly answers, correctly, "Yes." He is then asked, "What happened to the universe while God was dead?" In almost all instances, the answer is that it was not God who died upon the Cross, but the human nature of Christ. This is a form of the Nestorian heresy. It was condemned fifteen hundred years ago at the Council of Ephesus, but even educated Catholics still fall back upon it under pressure. I have said that this is the answer given by almost all. From time to time we get a different answer—"It was only the Second Person who died on the Cross, the other two survived and sustained the universe till His Resurrection." As a notion of the Blessed Trinity that reaches fantasy's limit.

I have chosen three examples from dozens, all illustrating the unhappy fact that Catholic laymen too often give no evidence of any grasp upon the doctrine of the Trinity, and certainly cannot win any other man to accept it. But the Trinity *is* God; what is not the Trinity is not God. The soldier of the Church is almost incapable of effective fighting unless he can do better.

There is one section of mankind in relation to which our failure to talk intelligently about the Blessed Trinity is especially shameful and especially disastrous—namely, the Jews. The Jew is a monotheist to the very marrow of his bones, and the doctrine of the Trinity stands as a lion in his path, precisely because it seems to deny the oneness of God to which through centuries and millennia he has clung. If he asks his Catholic friends about it, either they refuse to say anything at all; or else they embark upon an explanation which leaves him convinced that Catholics do in fact believe in three Gods, since they call the Father God, and the Son God, and the Holy Spirit God, while being totally unable to shed any light at all upon how these three can be one God.

I am not suggesting, of course, that every Catholic layman should be able to give a full theological exposition of either this or any other of the Church's dogmas. But he is failing as a soldier if he cannot talk of them intelligently, conveying enough of their meaning and their importance at least to arouse the other man's interest, and possibly make him willing to go to a priest for full instructions.

We are apt, we of the laity, to console ourselves with the assurance that theology is for the clergy, and that we do our duty by setting a good example. But it would be a very unusual soldier whose duty was only to set a good example. It is of enormous value that we should do so, but by itself it is not sufficient. Unbelievers are frequently impressed by the goodness and kindness and unselfishness of some Catholic who has come their way—impressed to the point where they wonder if his excellence may be due to something in his religion. So they ask him to explain his religion to them. If he answers intelligently and winningly, then the result is all good, the episode may end with the unbeliever receiving instruction from a priest. But if he talks nonsense, then the unbeliever can but depart, as sure as ever of that one Catholic's goodness, but convinced that his religion has nothing to do with it.

All experience seems to show that we of the laity do not teach very much truth to our acquaintances. What is more remarkable is that in our failure to teach we are not aware of any failure of duty. If in any group that happens to gather anywhere—in one's own town, or on a train or ship or airplane—there happens to be a Communist, everyone knows it at once. If there happens to be a Catholic, the chances are that no one ever discovers it at all. The Communist is consumed with a passion to spread the doctrines he holds true; the Catholic has no such passion. It is not that we love the Faith less than the Communist loves his Communism. There is another test of love besides willingness to win converts, namely willingness to die. And Catholics have always shown that willingness in most heroic measure. In those parts of the world where the Faith can be served today by dying, the Church has its martyrs. But in most parts of the world this is not so. What the Church needs from us is not our death but our witness, the witness of our life and our utterance.

Why do we of the laity fail to bear witness by utterance? Almost invariably the layman would like to speak out for the truth—not to win others to accept it, that thought hardly occurs to him, but at least to defend it against attack. Why is he silent? Usually, from a feeling that he does not know it well enough, that if he gets into an argument he will lose it. And this is probably true. But why is he not equipped for this most urgent duty? Because most Catholics see neither what the nature of the war is nor how they could help to win it.

Not to see facts so obvious means that they have not used their eyes. "If we do not use our eyes to see with, we will use them to weep with." The Church, we know, must triumph in the end. But in a given time and place it can be defeated. In our own time and place it does not look like winning.

For it takes no great military expert to predict the result of a war in which large numbers of the soldiers do not fight, do not even know that there is a war on. The officers are essential, and obedience to them is essential. But an army in which only the officers fight is likely to have no spectacular success in any war, least of all in this war which the Church is waging for the souls of men. For the great mass of the people we are fighting to win never meet an officer or hear an officer's voice. They meet us. It would be too much to say that they hear our voice.

2

A layman is not only a soldier, he is a man; as in all wars, the quality of his soldiering will depend upon the quality of his manhood. We have talked of what the Catholic should be doing to help others toward salvation. Let us now talk of what he should be doing in the field of doctrine for his own spiritual well-being, his growth as a member of the Body of Christ. We begin at the most elementary level.

Every man is a union of spirit and matter, of soul and body. So far there is no distinction between the layman and the priest, each has the same human structure, the same human needs. As a material object the body of a priest differs in nothing from the body of a layman. Each needs food, and will perish without it; each needs light and cannot see without it.

All that is so obvious that you may very well feel that I am carrying to an extreme my promise to begin at an elementary level. It seems too elementary to need saying at all. But it leads to something which is equally elementary, yet is not always realized by the laity. They know that as a material object a priest's body and a layman's do not differ. They do not always reflect that as a spiritual object a priest's soul and a layman's do not differ either. Each is a spirit which is the life principle in a body, each has the faculties of intellect and will, each is in contact with the exterior world through the body's senses. It follows that each has the same needs—the same personal needs, of course, not the same official needs. The priest has an office which the layman has not, and powers and duties that go with the office. But in what a soul needs merely because it is a human soul, there is no difference.

Thus, to take the most obvious example, all souls, lay and clerical, need baptism, confirmation, penance, Eucharist, extreme unction. Because of his special function in the Church, the priest needs holy orders; because of that other, lesser, function, on which all the same the continuance of the Church depends, the layman needs matrimony.

And all souls, simply because they are human souls, need truth, revealed truth. Because the priest has the official duty of teaching truth, he has a greater obligation to learn it and to master its utterance. But as a good for oneself, revealed truth is equally good for all souls, all alike suffer loss by not possessing it, or by possessing less of it than is available.

Truth is not simply a weapon to be used in warfare for the souls of others. It is food for the mind and light for the mind, our own mind is foodless and lightless without it.

It is food. To the Devil Our Lord quoted Deuteronomy— "Man does not live by bread alone, but by every word that proceeds from the mouth of God." The words God utters—commands for our action, truths for our seeing— are more life-giving, more nourishing, even than the bread which nourishes the body. For the intellect exists to know truth, and nothing else can nourish it; and the supreme truths are beyond its own, or any man's, power to discover. They can be known to the intellect, and therefore nourishing to the intellect, only if God reveals them. It is a peculiarity of food that it nourishes only those who eat it: we are not nourished by the food someone else has eaten. Only the truths which the mind itself has digested can nourish it. The theology which the theologians know does not nourish the layman until he, too, learns it. But his soul's *personal* need of nourishment is as great as theirs.

Thus truth is food. Truth is light too: possessing it, we see reality as it is, we live mentally in the real world. How are we to see reality as it is? The greater part of it cannot be seen by the eyes of the body at all. Our bodily eyes cannot see God, or the spiritual order, or the world to come. And though the mind, using only its natural powers, can see something of these, what it can see is still a small fragment of reality. The greater part can be known only if God reveals it. Those who do not know the things that can be known only by revelation are living merely in a suburb of reality; it is pathetic that they should think they are living in the whole of it.

Thus the man wholly cut off from revealed truth is living an unnourished life in the dark. The Catholic can never be in quite such poverty. He has the Blessed Eucharist for his nourishment; and something of the truths of Revelation he cannot help knowing. Yet insofar as he has not grasped the reality which the doctrines are meant to bring him, he is, at best, living an undernourished life in the half-dark. Between the unbeliever who does not accept the doctrine of the Trinity and the Catholic who accepts it but does not know what it means, the difference is not so great as we might wish. To accept the doctrine as true—and even to be devoted to it—but with no real grasp on what it means, makes it impossible to be nourished by it, impossible to gain light from it.

Religiously he is illiterate. Before the invention of printing, illiteracy was almost universal; even nobles, even kings, could not read; only the clergy could read. In the secular order that condition passed away. But in the religious order it remains—only the clergy can read. There are, of course, laymen who can, but they bear too small a proportion to the whole body to alter the general rule.

Religious illiteracy was bad enough when practically nobody was literate anyway. But what we have now is stranger and more dangerous. To be secularly literate and religiously illiterate produces an unbalance within the man. He finds himself with two eyes which do not focus—a strong eye which sees life as the world sees it, a weak eye which sees life as Faith declares it to be. The temptation is overwhelming to close one eye, the weak eye naturally.

It is not strictly necessary, we say defensively, for the layman to know theology. Only love is essential. But how can one love God and not want to know all one can about Him? Love desires knowledge, and knowledge serves love. Each truth that we learn about God is a new reason for loving Him. After all, the reason for loving God is not that our teachers love Him and communicate their love to us: it is that He is lovable; and we can know that He is lovable, only by knowing what He is. Love should flow into the emotions, it must not have its root in them. Love is not fully itself and invulnerable unless there is knowledge too.

What applies to love of God applies to all love—of Our Lord and His Mother, for instance. It applies to love of the Mass. The supreme function of the layman is the part he has—small compared with the priest's, but real—in offering the Mass. But how many of us see it as the supreme thing we do? Many of us feel it hardly worth going to Mass on a weekday if for some reason we cannot receive Communion.

Observe the phrase "going to Mass". It is miserably inadequate: it suggests that we do all that is required of us by being there. But we are not meant simply to sit and stand and kneel devoutly during the offering of Mass. We are meant to offer. And if we have not grasped what the Church has to teach upon the Blessed Trinity and the Incarnation and the redemption, we do not know *what* is being offered in the Mass, or *to whom* the offering is made, or *why*. We do not know what we are doing—an incredible condition for any offerer.

To return to our first question, what sort of a soldier will the uninstructed Catholic make? Stumbling along in the dark not even aware that it *is* dark, half-fed and not even hungry for more, he is in no state to show others the reality. Only a laity living wholly in reality is equipped to show it to others and win them to want to live in it too. That is the Church's warfare.